Temple and Tomb

Fresh Light on John's Gospel

Mark Fox

**SPIRIT
& SAGE**

2018

ISBN 978-0-9928197-3-6

Cover Designed by Teddi Black. Cover illustration: 'Solomon's Temple Jerusalem' http//Israeltruths.org/history/solomontemple.jpg, used under CCBY40/Filters used on the original.

Published by Spirit and Sage Ltd.

This book is dedicated, in loving memory, to my father, Edward Fox (1926-2017).

Author's Note

A book of this scope inevitably draws in several places on the work of others and a bibliography together with a full set of acknowledgements and references can be found at the end.

In keeping with convention, 'BCE/CE' rather than 'BC/AD' are used throughout, but they mean the same thing.

All bible quotations are from the English Standard Version (ESV) unless otherwise stated.

CONTENTS

Acknowledgements

Grateful thanks are due to many people who helped with the research, writing and completion of this book.

The fellowship at Kidderminster Baptist Church have been a continual source of encouragement and gave much positive feedback that encouraged me to turn what was initially an occasional series of talks into the chapters that make up this study.

Paul and Jean Mantle and Sally Bowen gave invaluable feedback at various stages of the writing process, providing encouragement and helpful insights at the very points at which I needed them.

Cherrill Mason kindly proofread the completed manuscript and made many helpful comments and corrections.

Teddi Black took my – very few – ideas and suggestions and turned them into the excellent front and back covers.

Last but by no means least: my wife, Trish, helped in so many ways that it is impossible to list them all here. Her love, help, encouragement and unfailing support were invaluable and made this project possible. Without her, *Temple and Tomb* would not exist.

Preface

I often wonder what it would be like to step out of a time machine and into Jesus' world. I try to picture myself standing at the controls: setting the co-ordinates for some time in the first few decades of the first century and stepping out into the noise and dust and tumult of first century Galilee or Jerusalem. Sometimes, the gospels – and particularly John's gospel – give such precise detail that it is hard to believe that their writers weren't there when Jesus said and did some of the things they tell us. There is such precision. There are names. There are places. And there are dates or things said and done that allow us to date *when* they were said and done. The very things needed to set a time machine for an exact historical arrival.

In my imagination I sometimes arrive in Jesus' world and Jesus is right there in the Temple at Passover with his disciples, turning over the tables of the money-changers, scattering cattle, and engaging in a furious argument with the indignant authorities. I drink in the sights and the smells, and although I don't understand a word of what I'm hearing I get the gist, because like all prepared time travellers I have chosen my co-ordinates with care. I know the history. I think I know something of what it means. I just want to see it for myself. And I want to see it as it happened.

The imagination might be capable of conveying us on wonderful journeys but, alas, the technology to travel in time still stands a long way off and most scientists tell us that it will never be possible anyway. So what's the next best thing?

The book that you hold in your hands started life as a series of talks given over an approximately five-year period in a variety of places. Usually I was invited to speak on a Christian theme but the choice of what that might be was left up to me and having a long-standing interest in John's gospel I naturally gravitated to that as a text I often spoke from. And having a long-standing interest in Jesus' Jewish background, I often drew from what I was learning about that as well. Slowly these two came together, with my research about Jesus' religious and cultural background informing my understanding of John's text. As a result - and rather to my surprise - I found my thinking and speaking converging on one central 'cluster' of points: the Temple in Jerusalem, what Jesus said about it, what he did when he was in it, and his relationship to it as described by John. The result was a series of talks with a common theme and that theme became the wellspring of this book.

The Temple at Jerusalem and Jesus' relationship to it has in recent years been a popular subject in the study of the New Testament. Today, it lies on the cutting edge of much interesting debate and discussion, but when I did my own degree and doctorate in Theology at the University of Birmingham several years ago it was a virtually unheard-of area. Now it is awakening much academic interest, yet as with so many academic 'hot topics' there is a significant gap between emergence within the cloisters of academia and arrival in churches and bookshops. Wanting to bridge the gap between academic research and a broader and more popular readership I decided to draw on the talks that I had already given and the result became *Temple and Tomb*.

Throughout, this book has a clear focus: to explore the relationship between Jesus and the Temple at Jerusalem as understood by John and to make this relationship clearly understandable to the interested reader and the non-specialist. As will become clear, John is an extremely subtle and gifted writer. His understanding of Jesus *as* the Temple is profound and largely unknown and yet it has incredible and far-reaching implications which we are only just beginning to understand. I invite you to join me as we journey back in time and as we peel back the layers of history, theology and archaeology in search of a profound and fascinating mystery and deep truth: a truth hidden for almost two thousand years by the sands of time.

Mark Fox

March 30th 2018

Introduction

The Passover of the Jews was at hand, and Jesus went up to Jerusalem. In the temple he found those who were selling oxen and sheep and pigeons, and the money-changers sitting there. And making a whip of cords, he drove them all out of the temple, with the sheep and oxen. And he poured out the coins of the money-changers and overturned their tables. And he told those who sold the pigeons, "Take these things away; do not make my Father's house a house of trade." His disciples remembered that it was written, "Zeal for your house will consume me."

So the Jews said to him, "What sign do you show us for doing these things?" Jesus answered them, "Destroy this temple, and in three days I will raise it up."

John 2: 13-19

A Curious Drama

Picture the scene. It is Passover and an angry man is causing mayhem in what is virtually the holiest place of his entire religion and culture. He is in the Court of the Gentiles, part of a massive space that surrounds the most sacred part of the Temple Mount, and he has chosen the time and the scene of his protest with care, for it is an area that comprises the most sacred space within the whole of Judaism and it is thronged with pilgrims and priests numbering in the tens of thousands, here to celebrate a holy festival of paramount importance.

This man has come prepared for what he will do, even to the extent of bringing with him the components of a whip with which to do it: wood for a handle and some simple leather strips which he attaches to it. And having assembled this crude device he uses it, driving sheep, oxen, and

1

men from the area. Then he pours the coins from the tables of the money changers onto the floor and orders the sellers of pigeons to take their wares and go. There is shouting and cursing and the sound of a small stampede. Then there is more shouting as those with responsibility for this sacred place challenge this clearly furious man to explain himself and to justify what he has done. The man flings back a reply, baffling his opponents with his words, creating yet more confusion. It is a tumultuous scene: violent, chaotic, noisy, and – for many – utterly baffling. Why has he done this? What gives him the right? And what does it *mean*?

The episode in which this man Jesus causes a disturbance in the Jerusalem Temple is one of the most vivid of any that we find in the gospels. In fact, it is one of a small number of episodes that we find in all four. In Matthew, Mark and Luke it occurs almost at the very end of his life, during his last visit to Jerusalem and very close to his eventual arrest and execution. But John presents a very different chronology and context. In *his* gospel, the episode occurs almost at the very beginning and shortly after Jesus has turned water into wine at Cana: the very first miracle that John describes.

How might we explain this striking difference between Matthew, Mark and Luke on the one hand and John on the other? Perhaps Jesus did this dramatic thing *twice*: once towards the beginning of his ministry, as recounted by John, and once towards the end, as recounted by Matthew, Mark and Luke. Or perhaps John is right and the others are wrong. Perhaps the others are right and John is wrong. Or perhaps John saw this act as so important that he deliberately placed it at almost the very beginning of his gospel: as a sort of key to help unlock the rest of it.

John certainly tells us a lot of things that Matthew, Mark and Luke do not. Only John describes the whip, the pouring of the coins onto the floor, the actual words of rebuke made specifically to the dove sellers – "Take these things away; do not make my Father's house a house of trade" – the apparent presence of disciples who will later remember the scene and the words used, the confrontation with the authorities, and the words that Jesus spoke as he spoke them: "Destroy this temple, and in three days I will raise it up." A somewhat different version of these strange words is found on the lips of some of Jesus' accusers at his trial as described by Matthew and Mark, but only John places them on Jesus' own lips at what is almost the climax of the entire drama.

What has come to be commonly referred to as the 'Cleansing of the Temple' is clearly an important episode for John. Locating it almost at the very beginning of his narrative and describing it with an eye for detail not found in the other gospels, it seems to point beyond itself, suggesting that it might be being used by this gospel writer as a lens through which to see much of what will follow in his work. Indeed, the simple whip of cords, a device only used on criminals and animals, prefigures a similar but far more fearsome instrument that we find at almost the very end of the gospel when a Roman whip – a *flagellum* - is used on Jesus himself prior to his crucifixion, whilst the enigmatic reference to 'three days' in Jesus' reply to his interrogators suggests that even at this early point in the gospel one of its most climactic scenes is being hinted at.

The Temple of his Body

It is little surprise that Jesus' actions in the Temple on this occasion – or on these occasions, if Jesus carried them out more than once – have inspired numerous painters. Most follow John, making the whip a prominent feature, and many capture vividly the violence and confusion of the scene.

In his *Christ Driving Merchants from the Temple*, for example, Jacob Jordaens portrays Jesus dressed in a red robe wielding the whip, the animal sellers and money-changers cowering under the angry onslaught. Tables are being scattered. Chaos reigns. But reactions are clearly mixed. The Temple authorities look on, puzzled but apart. A donkey gazes serenely at a scene of stampede and confusion. And a woman carries a basket on her head, her arm almost touching Jesus, but absolutely oblivious to the mayhem and his rage.

Giotto di Bondone's *Expulsion of the Merchants from the Temple* captures this mixture of reactions in a set of even starker contrasts. Jesus is central, wielding his whip at two traders while the cattle escape: a stark combination of simplicity and power. To the left the disciples converse among themselves: perhaps debating what the action means. To the right the Temple authorities converse also, but whilst they seem to share the disciples' puzzlement, they are shown in profile alone and appear to be conferring rather than simply conversing. Each painting captures vividly the range of reactions to what Jesus has done, but the *motif* of puzzlement is clear. It is, perhaps, a natural response to a wholly unexpected event. And it captures, too, not simply the consequence of Jesus' actions, but also his *words,* and once again, John provides the most detail concerning these. He has 'the Jews' asking of Jesus: "What sign do you show us for doing these things?" And Jesus, pointing forward to a sign yet to come, replies: "Destroy this temple, and in three days I will raise it up." At this point John intrudes, as he so often does: 'But he was speaking about the temple of his body. When therefore he was raised from the dead, his disciples remembered that he had said this, and they believed the Scripture and the word that Jesus had spoken' (John 2: 18-22).

So the temple in question is his body. But what does 'the temple of his body' actually mean? Is it no more than just an image or a euphemism for his physical self? Or does it mean something more? How might we best understand these words? In his gospel, John makes it clear that *nobody* apart from Jesus apparently understood them: at least, not at the time. What chance, then, do *we* have of understanding them? One possibility is that Jesus was acting and speaking not directly but *indirectly*, perhaps using the sort of riddle that rabbis of his day frequently used and hence using both his actions and his words – and particularly his claim to be a 'temple' - in a symbolic or analogical sense in order to invite deeper understanding on the part of his listeners. To this extent, he might be said to have eventually succeeded – at least with his disciples, whom John suggests eventually understood Jesus' words only after they had reflected after his death on what they had heard on that day. Certainly when we are invited to view a word or event in this way we are being invited to go beyond a merely surface interpretation of what is before us to grasp a depth that might reveal something different. In his description of Jesus' encounter with his opponents, John seems to be suggesting that they only fumble for some sort of surface meaning, and hence miss the deeper significance of what he did and said. But what might that significance be?

Twists and Turns

In the chapters that follow I will suggest that many of the actions and words of Jesus as they are presented in John's gospel are *more* than metaphors, analogies and symbols: particularly those associated with his teachings and actions that relate to the Temple. In fact, this book is about John as much as it is about Jesus, and its central focus will be the Temple. John is clearly very interested in the Temple, as well as Jesus' relationship to it, and this book will seek to explore what John's understanding of that relationship is.

Nobody likes a 'spoiler': particularly at the very beginning of a book. And as this one will take many twists and turns in its bid to uncover new clues which allow for a fresh understanding of John's gospel, it seems doubly inappropriate to give too much of the plot away before it has even begun. So, at the outset, I offer merely a taster of what is to come, in the hope that it might whet the reader's appetite for more. This book's core insight will be that John presents the incident in the Temple almost at the start of his gospel - and not, as in the case of Matthew, Mark and Luke, almost at the end – because it is fundamental to his own understanding of Jesus as *the* Temple. It is placed almost at the very beginning of his gospel by John because it unlocks so much of what follows. Indeed, by the time we get to John's presentation of this particular key we realise that it is one that has already turned and has, in fact, been present in his gospel from the opening verses. Throughout the chapters that follow, I will show that where John refers to Jesus in terms suggestive of the Temple it is because he sees those terms not as useful images with which to describe Jesus but as actual descriptions of what he was and is: and, crucially, what he *did* and *does*. If this is correct, it suggests that if we view the use of 'temple' and 'Temple' in John's gospel in a purely symbolic way we water down John's wine and miss the points he is trying to make. By contrast, what will become clear is that when John shows Jesus to be the Temple – and he does so throughout his gospel - he *means* it, and this has massive implications for our understanding of who Jesus was and is: implications which have not previously been properly explored or fully appreciated. It will therefore be this book's aim overall to both explore and appreciate this crucial insight, and to suggest ways in which this fresh appreciation of who John's Jesus was and is might impact all of our lives.

Why Here? Why Now?

Many people rightly have a long-standing suspicion of books that try to claim 'fresh', 'new' or 'original' insights into old mysteries. Can any new light be shed onto such things: particularly if, as in the case of John's gospel, we are dealing with mysteries and marvels wrapped in manuscripts that have been around for nearly two millennia and which have been turned over and examined on countless occasions? This book's response to this will be to say that yes, new light can indeed be shed on such things, and that at least three developments in recent decades have enabled this; providing, as they do, insights into Jesus and his world that simply did not exist before.

(1) Archaeology and the Temple

Since Israel's victory in the Six Day War in 1967 Jews now have direct access to the Temple Mount. The significance of this, whilst not always fully recognised, has been immense in a wide variety of ways, not least in allowing archaeologists unprecedented access to areas that had previously been denied to them. As a result, we now know far more than ever before about what life in and around Jerusalem was like in the days of Jesus, including life in and around the Temple, and this has in turn either confirmed what we already knew – from near-contemporaries of Jesus, such as the Jewish historian Josephus – or, in some instances, enabled entirely new discoveries. Archaeological discoveries elsewhere in the Holy Land, including those made outside of Jerusalem altogether, have added to our picture of what the Temple was like and – crucially – what its significance was for ordinary Jews in Jesus' day. We know, for example, that the Temple was revered in places like Galilee, and that Jesus and his disciples would have almost certainly shared that reverence. Its importance was acknowledged and its centrality to Jewish life and thought extended well beyond

6

Jerusalem: a crucial insight which may help to shed light on Jesus' sometimes dramatic actions within it and startling attitudes towards it.

(2) Jesus and Judaism

These archaeological insights are not the only things that allow us to look afresh at John's Jesus and his relationship to the Temple. It is now widely acknowledged that John's gospel, along with every other Biblical text, is something that you can ask critical questions about without surrendering your faith or in some sense sullying what you read. Whilst this approach to the Bible has been widespread within academic circles for nigh-on two centuries it has only been in comparatively recent times that it has found its widespread way into other places also. It is now quite common, for example, to find popular Christian books and publications asking searching and penetrating questions about what have historically been seen as 'untouchable' texts, and such questioning is now widely accepted as an ally – rather than as a threat to – faith.

Hand-in-hand with this development – and partly as a result of it – has been a greater appreciation of the central and crucial fact that Jesus was a first-century Jew and that such a recognition can add immeasurably to our understanding of who he was and what many of his actions and teachings meant and were intended, by him, to mean: including those centred on the Temple. In a crucial sense this has led to a profound shift in our understanding of Jesus. Nobody who reads the gospels – and John's gospel in particular – can fail to be struck by the hostility and name-calling that characterises his dealings with many of the Jewish authorities of his day. It certainly did not only occur when he turned over the tables and wielded his whip. Rather, it appears that 'the Jews' were forever arguing with him – and he with them. John, in common with the other gospel-writers, describes much plotting and scheming, angry words hurled by both sides, and a general air of mutual suspicion and distrust almost throughout his gospel. 'The Jews' insult Jesus, and at various points he insults them back: accusing them, on one occasion, of being children of the devil. They, in turn, plan and plot his death, and his eventual execution is portrayed as the eventual culmination of this. Little wonder, then, that Jesus has historically been understood in contrast to the Judaism of his times.

Yet this understanding of Jesus is almost completely wrong, and this is something else that has only relatively recently been acknowledged. Whilst there is little doubt that there was hostility between Jesus and his 'opponents', we now know that they had far more in common than has sometimes been supposed. His understanding of the law, his full immersion and engagement in Jewish life and ritual, the way he spoke and acted, the way he dressed; even the use of language, teaching techniques and idioms adopted by contemporary Jewish teachers of his day, all of these mark Jesus out as a profoundly and obediently Jewish male. Critical engagement with Biblical texts, including the gospels, has again permitted this fresh - and, for many, highly overdue – understanding, but other factors have been at work also. We now know, for example, that Judaism during Jesus' day was more richly diverse than was previously supposed, and we now recognise that the notion of a fixed, unchanging and monolithic first century religion called 'Judaism' is a grossly misleading one. We do better to speak of Judaism*s*, and to attempt to locate and understand Jesus within *these*.

(3) Jesus, Judaism and the Old Testament

Part of the reason behind this crucial insight has been the equally crucial insight that it is impossible to reconstruct first century Jewish life and thought using the Old Testament alone. Yet that is what has often been done and is, in fact, akin to trying to reconstruct the history of a people by using the barest fragments of evidence whilst ignoring an overwhelmingly massive collection of other things. As this book will seek to show – in part through the methods of enquiry that it adopts – there is much more to Jesus' thought-world than the Old Testament, and his view of the world was shaped by far more than this.

In Search of John

So there has never been a better time to try and shed new light on old questions and to revisit the answers to these that have traditionally been given and accepted, and this extends not just to Jesus but to those who knew and wrote about him as well. As has already been suggested, this book is in a crucial sense as much about the *author* of the gospel as it is about his principal character. As future chapters will make clear, the

Temple is, for John, the key to understanding Jesus. Such an understanding of his gospel has been almost entirely overlooked historically, and is rarely acknowledged even today, but it has a significant weight of evidence behind it. This book will present this evidence, examine it, and suggest that it enables us to see Jesus with new eyes.

Indeed, it will enable us to do more than this. As will become clear, the centrality of the Temple to John's gospel gives an additional clue to the identity of its *author*, in addition to shedding fresh light on his central character. Key facts, episodes and insights throughout his gospel make very clear that John was an eye-witness to many of the events he describes, and the nature of these details suggest, in turn, that he was present at many crucial times and places within the history that he narrates. Might this distinctive perspective and closeness to the action enable us to shed fresh light on John? Might he even be leaving deliberate clues as to his identity; clues which can be interpreted and explained by fitting them within the wider scheme of things within his gospel? We will see that both of these questions can be answered in the affirmative, once again by allowing the Temple to be the key that unlocks the gospel, and whilst these answers will almost certainly come as something of a surprise to those who thought the question of the identity of the author of the Gospel of John had been settled beyond doubt a long time ago, nonetheless they will be seen as justified by the evidence which John himself provides.

Methods and Approaches

As will have become clear, the focus of this book is very much on the Gospel of John. And John, of course, wrote more than a gospel. Three letters and Revelation all bear his name and Revelation also has the Temple at its heart. That this book does not consider these in any detail should not be seen as anything other than a simple recognition that the gospel is its key focus. Revelation, in particular, has a particular bearing on the conclusions that this book draws; indeed, in many key senses it reinforces them, but closer study of it will be reserved for elsewhere.

We are nearly ready to begin but before we continue it will be important to note two, final things. Firstly, in order to understand what John has to say about the relationship of Jesus to the Temple it will be necessary to say something about that Temple at the outset, and specifically about its history, meaning and importance both to Jews of Jesus' day and to Jews throughout previous generations. This, in turn, will require something of a 'detour' through history and as a result of this the opening couple of chapters of *Temple and Tomb* will have more to say about the Temple than they will do about John's gospel. The reader might like to bear this in mind, remembering that a detour is often necessary in order to reach a destination that cannot be reached in any other way.

Secondly – and finally - a word on what this book is *not* about. I am very aware that the reader can find elsewhere a significant body of literature that shares a concern to place the Temple at its heart. Specifically, I am talking about a very large body of studies that have historically sought in the Temple – and the Tabernacle before it – 'types' and prefigurings of the person, meaning and significance of Jesus. In this way, for example, the structure, materials, layout and content of both Tabernacle and Temple have been seen as historical 'forerunners' of him: as pointing toward him through the mists of history and as constituting imperfect 'copies' of what will only come to actuality and reality in and through him. That this book will not attempt anything like this will become clear early on. Whilst the Temple will be our focus, Temple typology *in this sense* will not be our concern. There are many such studies of Jesus. This book is not one of them.

Chapter 1: The Word Became Flesh and Dwelt Among Us

And the word became flesh and dwelt among us, and we have seen his glory, glory as of the only Son from the Father, full of grace and truth.

John 1: 14

Breaking All Records

It almost single-handedly coined the phrase 'epic of biblical proportions' and at the time of its release it was the most expensive film ever made. Making its box office debut on November 8th 1956 and filmed on location in Egypt, Sinai and the Sinai Peninsula, Cecil B. DeMille's *The Ten Commandments* was destined to break a string of box office records and was recently voted the tenth greatest epic of all time by the American Film Institute, putting it amongst an elite group of other Hollywood blockbusters and game-changers that includes Titanic, Spartacus, Gone with the Wind, Schindler's List, Ben Hur and Lawrence of Arabia. Featuring a cast of Hollywood legends including Yul Brynner, Charlton Heston, Anne Baxter, Edward G. Robinson and Vincent Price, *The Ten Commandments* remains one of the highest grossing films of all time and, when figures are adjusted for inflation, has to date earned the box office equivalent of 2 billion dollars at 2011 prices according to the Guinness Book of World Records. If 'epic' is a genre, The Ten Commandments largely defines it, and despite more recent remakes for both cinema and television it remains the greatest cinematic retelling of the events that unfolded when the Israelites escaped from Egypt and made their dramatic journey to the promised land.

Its makers boldly declared at the time of its release that *The Ten Commandments* was 'the greatest event in motion picture history' and the story it tells of the escape of the Israelites from Egypt - as recounted in the Bible's Book of Exodus - contains some of the most told and re-told stories in human, story-telling, history. Plagues, a dramatic sea crossing seemingly caused by a suspension of the laws of nature, miraculous provisions of food and water, incredible military victories: the earliest history of the group of escaped slaves under the leadership of Moses is rich in drama and excitement. It is fast-moving too. But when the Israelites reach Mount Sinai 'on the third new moon after the escape from Egypt' (Exodus 19:1) everything slows down. Detail intrudes. The newly-delivered people need laws. They also need to learn some things about the God who has delivered them. It will be Moses who will bring this divine-legal knowledge to them and who in so doing will be the intermediary through whom God will make a binding agreement with his chosen and newly-liberated people.

This story is incredibly important to John: particularly the story of what happened to the Israelites when they reached Sinai, stopped, met with God, and journeyed onwards with Him to the Promised Land. So important is it to him, in fact, that it is the very first Old Testament reference that he makes in his gospel: and he makes a lot. And, as this chapter will make clear, this is not merely a question of chronology. It is there at the very beginning of his gospel because it is a key – the first of many – that unlocks a lot of what will follow. When John writes, in words that are among the most often quoted in any gospel, that Jesus was the Word that 'became flesh and dwelt among us', he has the story of Moses and the Israelites in mind and he wants the reader to have it in mind as well. In order to appreciate this we will need to pause here in order to look at the events at Mount Sinai in more detail; particularly as they are described in the book of Exodus.

Fire on the Mountain

In a narrative that recounts the birth of Israel as a nation of chosen people governed by God-given laws, Exodus chapter 19 describes how, having escaped from Egypt amidst dramatic and miraculous events, the people pitch their camp in the wilderness at the foot of Mount Sinai. Moses then goes up alone and God calls to him, commanding him to remind the people of the events that they have already experienced and promising them that if they can keep His Law and the agreements that He will make with them they will be His 'treasured possession among all peoples' (Exodus 19:5). Moses goes back down the mountain and reports what God has told him, and the people agree to God's terms. God then tells him that the people must prepare 'for the third day': a momentous occasion when they will be able to come up with Moses to the mountain.

The people prepare as instructed and the third day dawns dramatically with thick cloud covering the heights and a deafening trumpet blast. Moses then leads the people out to meet God and smoke covers the mountain because God has descended upon it. Once again Moses speaks to God and God answers 'in thunder'. Then Moses goes ahead, back up the mountain to meet with God alone. Then God sends him back down to fetch his brother Aaron. Back and forth Moses goes – the sole intermediary through whom God addresses His chosen people from unapproachable heights. And it is as intermediary that Moses receives the Law in a series of climaxes that rise above the narrative like the peaks of mountains rise above a range: the Ten Commandments and the other laws, instructions and directives that the people of Israel will need to follow as a covenanted, consecrated, priestly nation.

God in the Midst

Up to and including the meetings of God with Moses on Mount Sinai the Book of Exodus is a numinously-charged narrative of drama, surprises, suspense and shocks, and as God delivers the Law through His chosen person to His chosen people it is difficult to believe that anything can surpass what has gone before. But there is yet another twist. Amidst the smoke and thunder of the mountain's heights, having met with Moses alone – and later, with a selected group of others including the elders of the people - God declares that henceforth He will dwell in the *midst* of the people and that when their journey resumes He will journey *with* them: immanently; at the heart of the camp. No longer will Moses go *up* to meet God. God will come *down* and will sojourn onwards with His people until their journey's end.

The crucial passage occurs in Exodus chapter 25. Here, God elicits via Moses a contribution from the people; a contribution of building materials necessary for this enterprise, before declaring that they shall "make me a sanctuary, that I may dwell in their midst. Exactly as I show you concerning the pattern of the Tabernacle, and all of its furniture, so shall you make it" (Exodus 25: 9). As God's instructions unfold concerning exactly how the Tabernacle is to be made, the rule seems to be: as above, so below. God's abode in the heavens will be recreated on the earth; His transcendence exchanged for a tent. It is an incredible development, one which will have profound implications throughout the rest of the story, and one which John draws richly upon as he sets out at the beginning of his gospel his profound and revolutionary understanding of who Jesus was.

Put simply: the Tabernacle was to be the set of arrangements by means of which God's presence would dwell at the heart of the Israelite camp. The God who descended from heaven to alight upon Sinai makes it clear that He will descend further still to join His people and camp in their midst, and this somehow in and through a set of portable structures and aided - and in some senses enabled - by what the priests will be told to do. Moreover, this set of arrangements was to be constructed according to a detailed list of instructions given to Moses, and as these unfold within Exodus chapters 25-30 it becomes apparent that God is directing Moses to follow what is nothing less than a blueprint: one set out in remarkable and exacting detail and which has been preserved for us in the Bible to this very day.

A Tent for a God Who Speaks

So it is that God instructs Moses and the people to assemble a set of structures that includes a tented central area within a courtyard containing an altar for sacrifice and a bowl in which priests must wash and purify themselves before entering the tent itself. Only priests are allowed into this tent, and only the High Priest – Aaron – will subsequently be allowed into one of its areas. It is, in fact, to contain two areas of unequal holiness, the holiest of which is to contain nothing but an acacia wood box overlaid with gold and topped by a cover – the 'mercy seat' - with a golden cherub at each end and intended to contain a small number of items including the tablets upon which the Law has been written. This box – the 'Ark of the Covenant', or 'Ark of Testimony' – is the place where God assures Moses that He will actually speak to him: "There I will meet with you, and from above the mercy seat, from between the two cherubim that are on the ark of the testimony, I will speak with you about all that I will give you in commandment for the people of Israel" (Exodus 25: 22).

The other part of the inner area – of less holiness and separated from the part containing the Ark by a veil – was to contain a table for bread, a golden lampstand and an altar for the burning of incense. Housing this divided inner area will be a tent, essentially: one consisting of curtains arranged on an acacia frame. Outside its screened entrance was to be the altar for sacrifice and the basin – or laver – for washing, and all screened from the rest of the camp by hangings of fine twilled linen.

Of crucial note is the fact that everything was to be constructed so that it could be *carried*, and there are detailed instructions for how this is to be done and by whom. It is above all a portable construction, designed to move as the people do, and the scriptures set out the precise set of arrangements through which God will move with them. Later in Exodus we read that it was all constructed exactly as God commanded. We are even told who made what. And we are told what the priests must wear, how they will serve, and how they are to be ordained. No detail is omitted: even down to how the anointing oil is to be made (Exodus 36-39).

It is clear from the description that the most important part of this complex layout will be the Ark. In fact, Moses' God-given blueprint begins with this and moves, as it were, from the Ark outwards. Clearly the Tabernacle is to be constructed for the sake of the Ark, and the whole for the sake of God and His indwelling presence in the midst of the people.

And so it comes to pass that the whole is completed down to the finest detail. Exodus chapter 39 – the book's penultimate chapter – ends with

Moses seeing all the work the people of Israel had done, 'and behold, they had done it; as the LORD had commanded, so had they done it. Then Moses blessed them' (Exodus 39: 43).

The climax comes in the very last chapter of Exodus. Here, having blessed the people, Moses erects the Tabernacle. The very last verses of Exodus make clear what happened next:

'Then the cloud covered the tent of meeting, and the glory of the LORD filled the Tabernacle. And Moses was not able to enter the tent of meeting because the cloud settled on it, and the glory of the LORD filled the Tabernacle. Throughout all their journeys, whenever the cloud was taken up from over the Tabernacle the people of Israel would set out. But if the cloud was not taken up, then they did not set out till the day that it was taken up. For the cloud of the LORD was on the Tabernacle by day, and fire was in it by night, in the sight of all the house of Israel throughout all their journeys' (Exodus 39: 34-8).

The Word Became Flesh

This dramatic and well-known story of God's journeying with His people Israel is uppermost in John's mind as he sets out the first eighteen verses of his gospel. It serves as a kind of 'backdrop' to it and, as will become clear, the reader cannot understand the beginning of John's gospel without at the same time being mindful of the events in Exodus which tower above it. The famous and much-discussed opening to his gospel is commonly referred to today as the 'Johannine Prologue' and can be usefully seen as a kind of 'map' through which John sets out from the beginning of his gospel a representation of a landscape that he will later 'fill in'. Like a good map, his Prologue allows the reader to get around what will follow. It shows the reader what to expect before he or she gets there. It shows the reader how to get around when he or she *does* get there. It points to things of particular interest and, more than that, to things of particular importance and significance. It provides orientation, guidance, and clarity, and in reading it the reader is helped to read everything else: the contours of the landscape, the things to pay attention to, and the things a traveller should not miss. The Johannine Prologue does all of these things, and John doesn't want anybody who intends to travel through his gospel to take a step further without having fully understood it. Indeed, so important is it that *we* cannot go any further in *this* study without considering it in detail. In words that have resonated throughout the last two thousand years of history, John writes:

'In the beginning was the Word, and the Word was with God, and the Word was God. He was in the beginning with God. All things were made through him, and without him was not any thing made that was made. In him was life, and the life was the light of men. The light shines in the darkness, and the darkness has not overcome it.

The true light, which gives light to everyone, was coming into the world. He was in the world, and the world was made through him, yet the world did not know him. He came to his own, and his own people did not receive him. But to all who did receive him, who believed in his name, he gave the right to become children of God, who were born, not of blood nor of the will of the flesh nor of the will of man, but of God.

And the Word became flesh and dwelt among us, and we have seen his glory, glory as of the only Son from the Father, full of grace and truth. For from his fullness we have all received grace upon grace. For the law was given through Moses; grace and truth came through Jesus Christ. No one has ever seen God; the only God, who is at the Father's side, he has made him known' (John 1: 1-5; 9-14; 16-18).

God Tabernacled Among Us

By the time we reach the end of the Prologue in verse 18 we have been introduced to a significant number of key themes within John's writing. Jesus is introduced as the 'Word'. He is presented as the One through whom everything was made, and as a light that is the life – the 'wellbeing' – of all people. He is shown to be one who will be rejected, yet at the same time as one who will be accepted too: by those, John tells us, to whom he will give the right to become children of God, born of His will. The only one who has ever seen God, Jesus is presented as the source of 'grace upon grace', the 'only begotten' from the Father, the one in whom a unique glory is beheld. But towering above every other one of this Prologue's incredible assertions, we recall its highest and greatest one. For this Word, John tells us, 'became flesh and dwelt among us.'

It would be easy to read this famous phrase as a way of saying that 'God became man' or 'God walked around among us', and it often *is* read in just this way. Yet, incredibly, John means more even than this. His use of the verb for 'dwelt' – *skenoo* – actually means 'to dwell in a tent' and is itself derived from the word for tent: *skene*. The choice of this word by John seems entirely deliberate. It was a word full of meaning for him and he presents it as part of his Prologue with great care. Among Greek-speaking Jews the noun *skene* was commonly associated with its derivatives such as *mishkan* (Tabernacle) and the better-known *shekinah*, which denotes the abiding presence of God. By choosing to portray Jesus as the divine tent-dweller John is clearly making an explicit – and early - reference to the Tabernacle traditions that we find in Exodus. 'The Word became flesh' therefore means far more even than 'God became a man' or 'God took on flesh'. 'God tabernacled among us' is favoured as a translation of verse 14 by some translators and is closer to the meaning that John wants to convey. 'Jesus became to us what the Tabernacle was to the Israelites' contains and conveys the fuller meaning. For John, Jesus was God's 'tented presence' on earth in the midst of His people. As we have seen, this is exactly what the Tabernacle was and what it allowed. It was the place of God's travelling presence and the point at which God dwelt and from which He directed operations within the Israelites' camp: including where the camp was to go. So Jesus-as-Tabernacle is on one level a powerful image with clear historic connotations and richly evocative of the time when God dwelt in the very geographical heart of His people, amidst the dust and drama of the Exodus, and throughout the Israelites' journey to the Promised Land.

More Than a Metaphor

It would be easy to grasp all of these things and to conclude that John seized on the image of the Tabernacle as a powerful symbol or metaphor to illuminate who Jesus was. Yet a further examination of what the Tabernacle did suggests that John means more than this. It is, in fact, as if John is trying to say that what the Tabernacle was Jesus was; and what it did, Jesus did. A final acknowledgement of the function of the Tabernacle lends weight to this interpretation, for, as we have already seen, the Tabernacle did not simply symbolise God's presence; it *was* God's presence. Where the Tabernacle was, God was. And in the Prologue, John appears to be suggesting that Jesus *was* this tented presence. As God descended from heaven to earth and then descended further to dwell in the midst of His people, so John makes clear did Jesus, as well.

Yet there is more, even, than this. We have already had cause to note that the Tabernacle was the point of God's revelation and that in Exodus God declares to Moses that He will speak to him from between the cherubim atop the Ark and this is very much in keeping with John's declaration at the beginning of his gospel as well. We recall the closing words of the Prologue that 'No one has ever seen God; the only God, who is at the Father's side, he has made him known.' Incredibly, John asserts that the tabernacling presence of Jesus reveals *more* than even Moses was permitted to see. 'For the law', he writes, 'was given through Moses; grace and truth came through Jesus Christ.' And in his declaration that 'we beheld his glory', John seems even to assert that he and others have seen what even Moses was not permitted to see. This suggests in turn that Jesus-the-Tabernacle is more than just a powerful image, and is instead a deeper and more powerful reality than even the original Tabernacle was.

So here, in the very opening verses of his gospel, John 'sets out his stall' and makes clear his agenda, using a powerful sign that is at the same time more than a sign. And although what this sign points to is as yet only hinted at, John will return to it again and again as his gospel unfolds, expanding and deepening it as he goes. In his Prologue, using a powerful image from Israel's history, he makes the startling claim that in Jesus God took on the same kind of reality in the midst of His people that He had previously done in and through the Tabernacle. In Jesus, says John, God camped in the midst of his people and revealed Himself to them, whilst providing the means for their forgiveness too: just as He had done generations before during the exodus. But the skin of this tent was no animal *skene*, slung on acacia wood poles. This was living, human, skin: the very flesh of a man born of a woman. In what follows, John will continue to develop this theme in vivid and at times startling ways. In equating Jesus with the Tabernacle he has alerted the reader to a significance and importance that goes to the very heart of who he thinks Jesus was and is, and he will have much more to say about it as his narrative unfolds.

Chapter Two: Angels Ascending and Descending

The next day Jesus decided to go to Galilee. He found Philip and said to him, "Follow me." Now Philip was from Bethsaida, the city of Andrew and Peter. Philip found Nathaniel and said to him, "We have found him of whom Moses in the Law and also the prophets wrote, Jesus of Nazareth, the son of Joseph." Nathaniel said to him, "Can anything good come out of Nazareth?" Philip said to him, "Come and see." Jesus saw Nathaniel coming towards him and said of him, "Behold, an Israelite indeed, in whom there is no deceit!" Nathaniel said to him, "How do you know me?" Jesus answered him, "Before Philip called you, when you were under the fig tree, I saw you." Nathaniel answered him, "Rabbi, you are the Son of God! You are the King of Israel!" And he said to him, "Truly, truly, I say to you, you will see heaven opened, and the angels of God ascending and descending on the Son of Man."

John 1: 43-51

Perchance to Dream

Human beings have always dreamed. In recent decades - and particularly in the Western world – a popular view of dreams is that they are merely the brain's clearing away of the mental rubbish and psychological detritus accumulated during the course of an average day. But this has by no means been the only way that *all* cultures – past and present – have understood dreams. In fact, the modern Western view seems to be the exception rather than the rule, and our ancestors seem to have viewed them as very much more than merely mental cleaning-up operations at day's end.

The Island of Kos was once home to the great healer Hippocrates, who, it was said, learned his skills at the island's asclepeion. This is no more than a magnificent multi-tiered ruin now, but in its day it was a powerful healing shrine: a complex of buildings to which sick supplicants would travel in the hope of receiving cures for their ailments. After undergoing a process of purification lasting several days in which they would bathe and adhere to a strict and specific diet, these pilgrims would make offerings and say prayers before being admitted by priest-physicians to the most important part of the asclepeion: the dream-chamber. Here, they would sleep in the hope of receiving a dream given by no less than the god Asclepius, said to be the Divine Physician. Many were said to receive diagnoses – rather than cures - in their dreams; diagnoses that were often couched in powerful, complex and symbolic forms. It was then the job of the priest-physicians to decode these disguised dream messages and to render them intelligible: to translate them into terms that would invite, in turn, appropriate cures. Like many modern psychologists, the priest-physicians were skilled dream-interpreters and trained in techniques that enabled them to 'translate' the dream-language into a formal medical diagnosis which would have been impossible to arrive at in any other way.

Travelling across Europe in the 1930s and 1940s, writer Lawrence Durrell came across a museum curator at the Kos asclepeion who warned him not to pitch his tent there because of the strangeness of the dreams that sleep would bring. Later, Durrell returned to the site and found a couple of soldiers who had camped there for a while before being forced to move on. They were, they said, unable to stay because of the vivid dreams that haunted their sleep and which they could no longer bear. It is tempting to speculate that the location of the Kos asclepeion – like other, similar, dream sanctuaries in the ancient world – was not chosen at random but had something to do with an understanding of the power of certain places to produce dreams that were vivid and significant - and sometimes disturbing too. This understanding of the power of the landscape to inform and to disturb has been all but lost today in our increasingly materialistic and non-mystical West but was common and widespread in ages and cultures gone by, as evidenced by the magnificent ruin that is the Kos asclepeion: an asclepeion which was once one of approximately three hundred such dream-sanctuaries that dotted the Greek and Roman worlds.

Dreams in the Bible

The Bible is full of accounts of unusual and frequently meaningful dreams, dreamed in unusual places and often in the midst of dramatic circumstances, and described in both Old and New Testaments. In the Old Testament, for example, the book of Genesis presents Joseph as one who dreams powerful and message-bearing dreams and who interprets both his own dreams and those of others, notably Pharaoh (Genesis 41: 1-36). In 1 Kings 3: 5-14 Solomon encounters God in a dream and is richly blessed because of the response he makes to the offer that God makes to him. In the New Testament, at the beginning of Matthew's gospel, it is information given by an angel in a dream that persuades Joseph not to divorce Mary when he discovers that she is pregnant; "because what is conceived in her is from the Holy Spirit" (Matthew 1: 20-1). Shortly afterwards the Magi are warned in a dream not to return to Herod (Matthew 2: 12). And even relatively unimportant biblical characters are given vivid and disturbing dreams with equally disturbing messages. Towards the end of Matthew's gospel, for example, Pilate's wife warns him to have nothing to do with Jesus, whom he is about to deliver to be crucified, "for I have suffered much because of him today in a dream" (Matthew 27: 19). Arguably, however, the most dramatic - and certainly the most vividly-described - Biblical dream is an Old Testament dream: that of Jacob, as described in Genesis chapter 28, verses 10-22.

"This is none other than the House of God!"

Jacob was the twin brother of Esau, the son of Isaac and Rebecca, the grandson of Abraham and Sarah, and the bible's narrative of his early life is dominated by the conflict that exists between him and his brother. Indeed, Genesis presents this conflict as occurring before the boys are even born, with Rebecca enquiring of God why the as-yet unborn twins are apparently contending together within her and receiving the answer that she has two nations in her womb (Genesis 25: 22-3). Later, when the boys are born, Jacob emerges grasping the heel of Esau, an event leading to his being named Jacob; literally, 'one who grasps the heel' (Genesis 25:26). This is but the start of the tension that exists between Esau, the first-born, and Jacob, his brother, and it is not long before Jacob tricks Esau into selling him his birthright, effectively obtaining the entitlement of his older brother to the physical belongings of their father along with the right to inherit the Promised Land. And just before his fateful dream, Jacob, with the help of his mother, deceives Isaac his father into bestowing his blessing on him and not on Esau: a reversal of what should rightfully have been the case given that Esau is - just about - the elder son. This irreversible decision is then discovered by Esau and naturally outrages him. Swearing to kill Jacob but postponing the deed out of respect for his father, it is clear that there is only one 'solution' that will leave both brothers alive: Jacob must flee. And this he does, ostensibly to seek a wife, but also to save his own skin (Genesis 27: 1-45). Thus it is that Jacob leaves his home for distant Haran. What happens next is both eerie and revelatory.

Coming to 'a certain place', Jacob decides to stay the night, the sun having gone down. He takes a stone, apparently to use as a pillow, and settles down for the night. Genesis 28: 12-15 tells the story:

> 'And he dreamed, and behold, there was a ladder set up on the earth, and the top of it reached to heaven. And behold, the angels of God were ascending and descending on it! And behold, the LORD stood above it and said, "I am the LORD, the God of Abraham your father and the God of Isaac. The land on which you lie I will give to you and to your offspring. Your offspring shall be like the dust of the earth, and you shall spread abroad to the west and to the east and to the north and to the south, and in you and your offspring shall all the families of earth be blessed. Behold, I am with you and will keep you wherever you go, and will bring you back to this land. For I will not leave you until I have done what I have promised you."'

Having dreamed, Jacob awakens and immediately realises the significance of his dream, together with what it means and what he must do. Genesis continues:

24

'Then Jacob awoke from his sleep and said, "Surely the LORD is in this place, and I did not know it." And he was afraid and said, "How awesome is this place! This is none other than the house of God, and this is the gate of heaven."

So early in the morning Jacob took the stone that he had put under his head and set it up for a pillar and poured oil on top of it. He called the name of that place Bethel, but the name of the city was Luz at the first. Then Jacob made a vow, saying, "If God will be with me and will keep me in this way that I go, and will give me bread to eat and clothing to wear, so that I come again to my father's house in peace, then the LORD shall be my God, and this stone, which I have set up for a pillar, shall be God's house. And of all that you give me I will give a full tenth to you"' (Genesis 28: 16-22).

"How awesome is this place!" In this exclamation Jacob shows himself well-aware that, despite the vividness of the detail of his dream, it is the *place* at which it occurs that is the important thing. It is a special location, and Jacob grasps its significance right away. It is nothing less than where God's house is, and thus the gate of heaven. And having grasped this, Jacob acts accordingly: taking the stone, he makes his pillow into a pillar and anoints it with oil, thus turning the place into a shrine. But not just any shrine. The name Bethel itself discloses the significance of the place both for Jacob and, by extension, for the reader of the text. It is literally *Beth-El*: the House of God. Not *a* house: *the* house.

How did Jacob know that this was the House of God? Perhaps it was the feeling with which he awoke or which his dream evoked when he remembered it. Genesis says that his first feelings upon awakening were those of fear and awe. But why associate these feelings with the conviction that he was at the very place where God's house was? One very obvious clue is contained within the dream itself, and specifically in its incredible tableau featuring a ladder that stretched all the way from earth to heaven with angels ascending and descending on it and God at the top, re-affirming promises already made to Jacob's

25

ancestors but now declaring them to Jacob himself. Jacob – and any reader, come to that - could be forgiven for thinking that such a place, where earth and heaven were joined and God declared His covenant and will, would surely be a very powerful candidate for being the place where God dwelt. Indeed, as we saw in the last chapter, this was the very role that the Tabernacle performed, being nothing less than God's dwelling place on earth, the place where heaven and earth met, and a 'portable Sinai' from which God, dwelling amongst His people, declared His sovereign will.

'I Have Built for You an Exalted House'

After Israel entered the Promised Land, many years after Jacob's dream-encounter at Bethel, Joshua renewed the covenant with God that Moses had made at Sinai. When the Israelites had consolidated their hold on the land, the Ark – and, one assumes, the Tabernacle that housed it – was set up at a place called Shiloh. Later, by the time of the Judges, it was at Bethel. It was then stolen by the Philistines but returned in dramatic circumstances and taken to the house of Abinadab in Kiriath-Jearim. After the death of King Saul, David became king and one of his first acts was to bring the Ark to Jerusalem. But tragedy struck. The Ark was put on a cart and when this became unsteady Uzzah reached out to try and steady it and was struck down. Clearly, the Ark had lost none of its holy, vicarious and inexplicable power. David, both angry and fearful, then left it for three months in the house of Obed-Edom the Gittite. Then it was brought to Jerusalem and placed in a tent. And whilst David wanted to build a Temple within which to house it – a proper House for God's presence, in effect - this was only finally realised after his death by his son, Solomon.

The location at which Solomon finally built the Temple was Mount Moriah in Jerusalem: where the Temple Mount still stands. This was then and is now a place pregnant with history, being the place where Jacob's grandfather Abraham was commanded by God to sacrifice his son Isaac in a test of faith. Solomon's original Temple took seven years to build but was eventually completed and dedicated, with the Ark being housed within its Holy of Holies, as it had been within the

Tabernacle. Indeed, the ground plan of the Temple matched that of the Tabernacle, because naturally the Temple, like the Tabernacle before it, needed to be built strictly according to God's instructions. Thus, as the Tabernacle contained a Holy Place and a Holy of Holies, with the former restricted to priests and the latter restricted to the High Priest (and then only once a year, on the Day of Atonement) so too did the Temple. The altar of incense, seven branched candlestick and table of showbread were all in the Temple's Holy Place, just as they had been in the Tabernacle's. The altar of sacrifice was outside the entrance also, as was the laver for the washing of the priests. Indeed, apart from its dimensions, the Temple effectively *was* the Tabernacle, with the exception that whilst the latter was portable the former was fixed.

When the Temple was completed, it was dedicated to God. And once again, as with the Tabernacle, the climax of the Temple's construction and dedication was the entry of the glory of the Lord into the Holy of Holies. 1 Kings 8: 6-21 tells the story:

> 'Then the priests brought the ark of the covenant of the LORD to its place in the inner sanctuary of the house, in the Most Holy Place, underneath the wings of the cherubim. For the cherubim spread out their wings over the place of the ark, so that the cherubim overshadowed the ark and its poles...And when the priests came out of the Holy Place, a cloud filled the house of the LORD, so that the priests could not stand to minister because of the cloud, for the glory of the LORD filled the house of the LORD.'

> 'Then Solomon said, "The LORD has said that he would dwell in thick darkness. I have indeed built you an exalted house, a place for you to dwell in for ever." Then the king turned round and blessed all of the assembly of Israel, while all the assembly of Israel stood. And he said, "Blessed be the LORD, the God of Israel, who with his hand has fulfilled what he promised with his mouth to David my father, saying, 'Since the day that I brought my people Israel out of Egypt, I chose no city out of all the tribes of Israel in which to build a house, that my name might be there. But I chose David to be over my people Israel.' Now it was in the heart of David my father to build a house for the name of the LORD, the God of Israel. But the LORD said to David my father, 'Whereas it was in your heart to

build a house for my name, you did well that it was in your heart. Nevertheless, you shall not build the house, but your son who shall be born to you shall build the house for my name.' Now the LORD has fulfilled his promise that he made. For I have risen in the place of David my father, and sit on the throne of Israel, as the LORD promised, and I have built the house for the name of the LORD, the God of Israel. And there I have provided a place for the ark, in which is the covenant of the LORD that he made with our fathers, when he brought them out of the land of Egypt.'"

Thus did the tent become, finally, a house: God's house.

Bethel or Jerusalem?

There is, of course, an issue of geography here. Whereas Jacob realised as a result of his dream of angels ascending and descending that he had almost literally stumbled over the location of God's house in Bethel, the Temple built by Solomon was located on Mount Moriah, in Jerusalem, some way south of Bethel, and therefore at a different location altogether. How to reconcile this difference? How could God's house be at both Bethel *and* Jerusalem, when both places were geographically removed from each other?

Within Jewish tradition this has historically not been seen as an insoluble problem. In fact, the site of Jacob's dream is frequently ascribed to Mount Moriah, with Jacob's altar being seen as the 'forerunner' of the Holy of Holies in Solomon's Temple. Thus, when God promised Jacob the land of Israel, some traditions have it that he actually did so in Jerusalem. The Hebrew text says that Jacob came not to '*a* place', but to '*the* place' (*vayifga bamakom*), and some early sages interpreted this as a reference to Jerusalem. After all, where else could *the* place possibly be? This is where the Talmud locates it, and the Talmud contains traditions that go back to Jesus and before. Of course, locating Jacob's dream at Jerusalem rather than Bethel would require both ingenious exegesis of the text and something akin to miraculous transformation of the landscape, and we find both in the writings of the great and renowned medieval Jewish scholar Rashi who suggests that Mount Moriah united with the mountain at Bethel for just one time in all of history: the very time when Jacob dreamed his dream.

What is absolutely clear is that a number of phrases in the Genesis narrative relating to Jacob's dream – 'House of God', 'gateway to heaven', 'awesome place' – are clear references to the later Jerusalem Temple on Mount Moriah: the place that Jesus himself visited and taught at on many occasions during his lifetime. This is vividly reflected in the 1 Kings dedication passage with its repeated references to 'the house of the LORD', 'exalted house', 'a house for the name of the LORD', and so on. It is equally clear that the geographical inconsistency has provided no problem for sages and readers down the ages who have been keen to understand the overall meaning of the Genesis story of Jacob's dream. Rabbinic biblical interpretation in particular has proved easily flexible enough to either reconcile the differing locations of Bethel and Jerusalem or to simply ignore the problem altogether. Certainly, any Jewish reader in Jesus' day would have had no more of a problem understanding the significance of Jacob's dream than Jacob himself did. Put simply, they would know: wherever you see angels ascending and descending you are at the very point where heaven and earth meet. Therefore (and crucially, hence the italics!): *angels ascending and descending mark the very spot where the Temple is and where God's presence dwells.* Jacob set up a crude stone forerunner to the Temple that Solomon eventually built at the point where he dreamed his dream of the ladder. The ladder that leads from heaven to earth is thus rooted in the very spot where the Temple is, the spot where Jacob erected a pillar and anointed it at the gate of heaven, and angels ascend and descend upon it as they move between the soil below and the heavenly places above.

'What Are You Seeking?'

In his Prologue, John tells us that Jesus, and not John the Baptist, was the true light that came into the world. John, he says, came to bear witness to the light, and in verse 29, shortly after the end of the Prologue, he does just that, declaring Jesus to be no less than the Lamb of God who will take away the world's sins: a designation that will be of enormous importance by the end of the gospel, as we will see. John the Baptist makes a very similar assertion shortly afterwards, in verse 36, but this time in the company of two of his disciples. It is at this point that these disciples effectively transfer their discipleship and allegiance, leaving John to follow Jesus. The story is well worth considering in full:

'The next day again John was standing with two of his disciples, and he looked at Jesus as he walked by and said, "Behold, the Lamb of God!" The two disciples heard him say this, and they followed Jesus. Jesus turned and saw them following and said to them, "What are you seeking?" And they said to him, "Rabbi" (which means Teacher), "where are you staying?" He said to them, "Come and you will see." So they came and saw where he was staying, and they stayed with him that day, for it was about the tenth hour. One of the two who heard John speak and followed Jesus was Andrew, Simon Peter's brother. He first found his own brother Simon and said to him, "We have found the Messiah" (which means Christ). He brought him to Jesus. Jesus looked at him and said, "You are Simon the son of John. You shall be called Cephas" (which means Peter)' (John 1: 35-42).

This episode is typical of the gospel of John and we do well to pause to consider its nuances, subtleties, and motifs. In explaining that 'Rabbi' means 'Teacher' John seems to have a readership for his gospel in mind that may not be acquainted with even the basics of Jewish tradition. Either this, or an originally very Jewish text has been annotated for a wider, non-Jewish audience. Indeed, the writer of John's gospel is frequently designated by commentators as an 'intrusive narrator'; one who 'buts in' to the narrative on numerous occasions to clarify concepts, places and terms for readers who may not be familiar with them, and this intrusion is repeated over and over again throughout the gospel (usually placed in brackets by the translators).

John also tells us that these disciples came and stayed with Jesus 'about the tenth hour', suggesting that he is either an eye-witness to the events he is describing or has received them from somebody else who was. Shortly afterwards we learn that one of these two disciples was

Andrew, Simon Peter's brother, who then finds his brother to tell him that they "have found the Messiah." Having been brought to Jesus by his brother Andrew, Jesus gives Simon a new name: Cephas, which is translated for the reader as Peter.

John then goes on to describe what happened 'the next day'. Deciding to leave for Galilee, Jesus finds Philip and asks him to follow him and a complex series of exchanges follow. Jesus' decision to move to Galilee is interesting; highlighting, as it does, the fact that the 'action' in this gospel shifts from place to place, and that places are important. More than any other gospel, however, and in contrast with its Galilean 'incidents', John's gospel has a particular concern to detail events in Judea and in and around Jerusalem. The reason for this becomes clearer as the story continues:

> 'The next day Jesus decided to go to Galilee. He found Philip and said to him, "Follow me." Now Philip was from Bethsaida, the city of Andrew and Peter. Philip found Nathaniel and said to him, "We have found him of whom Moses in the Law and also the prophets wrote, Jesus of Nazareth, the son of Joseph." Nathaniel said to him, "Can anything good come out of Nazareth?" Philip said to him, "Come and see." Jesus saw Nathaniel coming towards him and said of him, "Behold, an Israelite indeed, in whom there is no deceit!" Nathaniel said to him, "How do you know me?" Jesus answered him, "Before Philip called you, when you were under the fig tree, I saw you." Nathaniel answered him, "Rabbi, you are the Son of God! You are the King of Israel!" Jesus answered him, "Because I said to you, 'I saw you under the fig tree', do you believe? You will see greater things than these. And he said to him, "Truly, truly, I say to you, you will see heaven opened, and the angels of God ascending and descending on the Son of Man"' (John 1: 43-51)

Here, having told us that Philip, Andrew and Peter are all from Bethsaida, John then goes on to tell us that Philip 'found Nathaniel' to tell him that they, in turn, had "found him of whom Moses wrote about in the Law, and about whom the prophets also wrote, Jesus of Nazareth, the son of Joseph". Nathaniel is clearly surprised by this announcement: not, as might be expected, because of its momentousness, but by the fact that such a person of whom Moses and the Prophets wrote could have come from a relative backwater like Nazareth. Betraying his surprise, he asks "Can anything good come from Nazareth?" and in so doing may have been giving expression to a popular saying of the time and preserved for always by John. Philip's response to Nathaniel's surprise is a simple "Come and see" and Jesus' subsequent reaction to Nathaniel's approach is an interesting one. He says: "Here is a true Israelite, in whom there is nothing false", and it is tempting here to view this description as standing in sharp contrast to what might have been said about Jacob, the deceiver, fleeing to Haran to escape the consequences of his trickery. Nathaniel's response to what on the surface appears like a compliment is an interesting one too, but its straightforwardness suggests that Jesus' summary of his character is accurate. "How do you know me?" Nathaniel replies, and Jesus now surprises Nathaniel by telling him that he saw him under the fig tree before Philip called him. Nathaniel's reaction to this is to declare that Jesus is "the Son of God...the king of Israel." But it is Jesus' reply to this declaration - forming, as it does, the climax of the narrative - that is most interesting. "You believe because I told you I saw you under the fig tree", he says, before adding: "I tell you the truth, you shall see heaven open, and the angels ascending and descending on the Son of Man."

Heaven Opened

This latest development is no surprise, given what John has already told us in his gospel's Prologue. In addition, its meaning would certainly be understood by anybody familiar with the content and significance of Jacob's dream. It is important, however, to be clear about exactly *what* is being claimed. That the phrase "[Y]ou shall see heaven open, and the angels ascending and descending on the Son of Man" is supposed to direct the reader to the incident of Jacob's dream is beyond doubt. The imagery is specific, striking, and obviously deliberate and it is tempting to conclude from this passage's climax that Jesus' words equate to something like: "As with Jacob, so I too am a figure upon whom God's favour rests and through whom the world will be blessed". And whilst this is certainly implied, it is already clear by the end of the first chapter of this gospel that *more* is meant. We have already seen Jesus vividly equated with the Tabernacle. Now we see him as the Temple. Recalling to the reader's mind the vivid episode in which Jacob was allowed to discern where the Temple was, Jesus at the climax of this chapter makes the bold claim that *he* is the point upon which the ladder to heaven rests: that he is, in fact, that very location where the angels ascend and descend. Anything less than this fails to do full justice to Jesus' claim and to the continuity that exists between it and what John has already drawn clear attention to in his Prologue. It is an absolutely natural and logical progression. Just as Jesus has been revealed to be the Tabernacle, now he is being revealed as the Temple. Indeed, he could hardly have been the one without being the other, given that in specification, function, and detail, they were effectively the same.

Pressing On

If you have ever taken part in a marathon, half-marathon, or other run over distance you will know how encouraging it is to hear shouts urging you on: particularly at those times when you feel that you still have quite a way to go. The last two chapters of this book have said much about the Tabernacle and Temple and comparatively little about John's gospel and you may be wondering at this point how far you have to go before the 'main event' will actually start! If so, the message to you at this point is: keep going!! This book has much more to say about John's distinctive portrayal of Jesus and most of that lies ahead. The problem – if 'problem' in the right word – that any writer or commentator on John's gospel has is of conveying in sufficient detail the first-century Jewish context that is so fundamental to a full understanding of the wealth of meaning presented in his account of Jesus' actions and words. As the Temple, and in particular its centrality and significance for the Jewish people at the time of Jesus and before, is so crucial a part of that context for John, it has been necessary to chart its origins, history and importance in some detail at the outset. We are, however, in a much better position now to understand what John intended to tell us in his gospel when he wrote it. Equipped with this understanding, it is now time to wade into the thick of the action in John's gospel and to return to take a closer look at one of its most dramatic events: Jesus' remarkable words and actions on that Passover day when he drove the cattle and money-changers from the Temple courts and claimed, in the clearest possible terms, to *be* the Temple which he was cleansing.

Chapter Three: 'But the Temple He Had Spoken of Was His Body...'

The Passover of the Jews was at hand, and Jesus went up to Jerusalem. In the temple he found those who were selling oxen and sheep and pigeons, and the money-changers sitting there. And making a whip of cords, he drove them all out of the temple, with the sheep and oxen. And he poured out the coins of the money-changers and overturned their tables. And he told those who sold the pigeons, "Take these things away; do not make my Father's house a house of trade." His disciples remembered that it was written, "Zeal for your house will consume me."

So the Jews said to him, "What sign do you show us for doing these things?" Jesus answered them, "Destroy this temple, and in three days I will raise it up." The Jews then said, "It has taken forty-six years to build this temple, and will you raise it up in three days?" But he was speaking about the temple of his body. When therefore he was raised from the dead, his disciples remembered that he had said this, and they believed the Scripture and the word that Jesus had spoken.

John 2: 13-22

Approaching the Temple

Imagine the scene. You are one of Jesus' disciples on that incredible day when he turns over the money changers' tables and drives the cattle from the Temple courts. It is Passover and Jerusalem is thronged with pilgrims. It is noisy and crowded and the air is filled with talking and praising. You wonder how the city can hold so many people as you make your way from your temporary encampment outside of the walls and through the Holy City itself, still unsure of what the day will bring,

35

but knowing where your ultimate destination will be, for the Torah – the Law of Moses - requires you to be at the Temple, and your rabbi is leading the way. In the time that you have known him he has both delighted and confounded you, encouraging you as you attempt to walk in his footsteps and imitate his way of living, but chiding you when you have been slow to understand his teaching. Sometimes what he says seems to make no sense to you at all, and you have begun to suspect that there are things that you will not fully understand until you have walked with him a good deal further.

You are talking quietly with your fellow-disciples as, following rabbi Jesus, you make your way through the south of the city. Something is in the air: you all sense it, and your excitement mixes with trepidation as you approach the main entrance façade of the vast Temple complex. Together with your rabbi and the other disciples you have already purified yourself, ready to go as close to the Temple's holiest places as the law permits. You have descended stone steps into a bathing pool - one of a number of such pools, or *miqva'ot* that surround the approach to the Temple courts – and having descended into it by one set of steps you have immersed yourself in its water before climbing back out again via another set of steps: ritually pure, now, and ready to proceed. It is a ritual that you have undergone many times and it is as familiar to you as the route to the Temple itself. You know that to gain access to the Temple courts you will need to climb a vast stairway and then ascend by yet more steps as you enter the sacred space of the Temple Mount. Moving through the Royal Portico and into the vast space beyond, you will on several previous occasions have seen the signs warning in the clearest possible terms of the consequences that will befall any non-Jew who attempts to go beyond this point: for here is the Court of the Gentiles, the furthest part of the Temple Mount that non-Jews are permitted to access. In this area there is nothing short of controlled chaos, with the Temple guards barely able to maintain order. The noise of bellowing and shouting combines with the stench of animals and the flashing of coins in the brilliant sunlight because this vast space is where ritually clean and approved animals are sold for sacrifice and where varieties of coins and currencies are exchanged for coins that do not bear an idolatrous image of the Emperor or King on them. Coins, in other words, which are 'clean' and hence fit for the purpose of paying the Temple Tax. And everything must be checked and approved: even you.

To the Heart of the Sanctuary

But you are an observant Jew and thus permitted to move beyond this area. Again, it is a route you have travelled many times on your previous Temple visits. You know that Solomon's Portico stands at the East of the Temple Mount. In fact, this is a place that your rabbi, Jesus, particularly likes, and you have sat at his feet many times in this area, sometimes facing West where the Court of the Women stands with its trumpet-shaped collection boxes for the depositing of Temple offerings. At the Western end of this court stands the Nicanor Gate. You have previously passed through it on several previous visits to the Temple on your way to the Court of the Israelites and beyond it you can see the Altar of Sacrifice and the entrance to the heart of the Temple itself with its Holy Place and its Holy of Holies.

Today, however, you will not get far into the Temple complex. In fact, you will not get any further than the vast Court of the Gentiles. For here, amid the people using its space to take short cuts across the city and surrounded by the bellowing and the snorting and the shouting and the clinking of coins, your rabbi will do things and say things that you will only understand in the future when you have lived through events so dreadful and wonderful that they will change your life forever.

From Solomon to Herod

On this visit to the Temple it will not have been the Temple built by Solomon that you will have visited. In fact, only the location will have been the same. After Solomon's death things were to change in the Kingdom of Israel and the dramatic chain of events that subsequently convulsed the land and which played out over many centuries after his reign ended was to have a massive impact on the Temple he established, leading ultimately to its destruction and eventual re-building. At the time of his death in 931 BCE Israel was both expansive and united but shortly afterwards it became split into two Kingdoms: the Northern Kingdom of Israel with its capital at Samaria and the Southern Kingdom of Judah with its capital at Jerusalem. The Northern Kingdom fell to the invading Assyrians in 722/1 BCE and its inhabitants carried off into captivity – a well-known tactic to ensure the breaking of any remaining national resistance. It was only a matter of time before the Southern Kingdom would suffer a very similar fate at the hands of another dominant power. By 609 BCE Jehoiakim was King of Judah and he rebelled against the mighty and feared Babylonians. He was succeeded by his son Jehoiakin and it was during his reign that the Babylonians unleashed their brutal wrath. They besieged Jerusalem, his capital, before taking it in March 597 BCE. Apart from the poorest and weakest, the victorious invaders carried everyone off into captivity as the Assyrians had before them, installing Zedekiah as king over Judah and Jerusalem. But Zedekiah did not remain loyal. Rebelling against the Babylonian occupiers, his actions were to lead to the eventual destruction of both Jerusalem and the Temple by Nebuzaradan, the captain of Babylonian King Nebuchadnezzar's bodyguard. As 2 Kings 25 verse 9 graphically and starkly puts it: 'And he burned the house of the LORD and the king's house and all the houses of Jerusalem; every great house he burned down'.

A Second Temple

But empires rise and fall, and the fortunes of peoples with them. After the establishment of the succeeding Kingdom of Persia, Cyrus, the king, made a proclamation in 529 BCE permitting the Israelites to return to their country to rebuild their Temple. Yet the Temple they built when they returned was at the outset a very poor shadow of the former one's Solomonic splendour. For one thing, it appears not to have contained the Ark. And Ezra 3: 12 gives a graphic description of the mixed feelings that this second Temple evoked as its foundations were being laid: 'And all the people shouted with a great shout when they praised the LORD, because the foundation of the house of the LORD was laid. But many of the priests and Levites and heads of father's houses, old men who had seen the first house, wept with a loud voice when they saw the foundation of this house...'

Nonetheless, the return from exile and the re-establishment of the Temple on Mount Moriah marked the beginning of a virtually unbroken period of its existence and daily operation that was to extend for approximately 600 years: an astonishing length of time. With the exception of a very brief period in the second century BCE the daily and annual rites and rituals of prayer, praise, sacrifice and ritual never ceased. But whilst the site and functions of the Temple remained unchanged, the Temple complex on Mount Moriah had grown massively by the time of Jesus and would have been unrecognisable by those returned exiles who had shouted and wept at the laying of its foundations over five hundred years before.

The Temple Jesus Knew

In 20-19 BCE some seventeen years after his accession to the throne, Herod, King of Judaea, began a massive and unprecedented programme of Temple expansion and elaboration. And what has come to be referred to as 'Herod's Temple' – or the 'Second Temple' - is the one that Jesus and his disciples visited on the day that we have still to fully consider: the day when he strode through the Court of the Gentiles with his hand-made whip of cords. We know a considerable amount about this Temple, thanks to a rich range of sources. We have the writings of the historian Josephus, for example, who came from a priestly family and knew it well and describes it in detail in works such as *Antiquities*, *The Jewish Wars*, and *Against Apion*. We have detailed descriptions of its dimensions and operations in the *Mishnah* and in particular *Mishnah Middot*, part of a detailed set of rabbinic writings that includes material from the period when Jesus lived. We have a wealth of archaeological evidence going back several centuries and which has expanded considerably since modern archaeological access to the Temple Mount was facilitated in the aftermath of the 1967 Six-Day war. We also have the gospels, which include a wealth of material to do with the Temple that stood in the early decades of the first century. And whilst, as we have been seeing, it is John who has the most to say about this Temple, the other gospels are by no means lacking in detail.

One little episode found in Matthew, Mark and Luke is particularly revealing. As Mark tells it, Jesus and the disciples are coming out of the Temple. Previously, Mark has told us about a poor widow who has put two copper coins – 'everything she had' – into the offering box and been commended by Jesus for doing so (Mark 12: 41-4). Emerging from the Temple, one of Jesus' disciples – we are not told who – remarks to Jesus: "Look, Teacher, what wonderful stones and what wonderful buildings!" (Mark 13: 1). The distinction between stones and buildings is an interesting one. Why not just comment on the grandeur of the *buildings*? Why distinguish them from the stones? After all, it would be difficult to conceive of them without their being made out of *something*. But an examination of our evidence – historical and archaeological – answers these questions. It was, indeed, not just the buildings that were staggering in their dimensions. The stones were too. In fact, the largest of them has been compared to a city bus; bigger than anything in the Great Pyramid at Giza. One still extant stone from the Western retaining wall has been measured at 13.7 metres wide, 3.5 metres high, and approximately 4.5 metres wide. Its weight is estimated to have been heavier than even the heaviest stone of any of the pyramids. Given these facts, it would indeed have been natural to remark on the stones as well as the buildings.

'What Wonderful Buildings!'

But the buildings themselves were remarkable as well. Herod's ambitious Temple-building programme included expansion of the Temple Mount – the platform upon which the Temple buildings stood – on three sides. Only the Kidron valley prevented him from expanding it on a fourth side as well. And whilst the inner sanctuary comprising the Holy Place and the Holy of Holies was only 36.5 metres wide and just under 41 metres long (and its location identical to that of Solomon's temple), the buildings and complex around it expanded the Temple's total area massively. It has been hailed, in fact, as the greatest architectural achievement of the Greco-Roman world and was, as far as is known, the largest temple in the ancient world, being approximately twice the size of Trajan's (slightly later) Roman Forum. By the time of Jesus it was capable of accommodating a stunning one million people. It has been estimated that the workforce required to build it would have numbered 10,000 men of which 1,000 were priests: the only persons allowed to participate in the construction of its holiest parts. To create a platform big enough to create a stage for his archaeological ambitions, Herod effectively 'boxed in' the highest part of Mount Moriah. The resulting stone box was approximately the size of six football fields, and the whole thing was linked to the rest of Jerusalem by a massive overpass that weighed over 1000 tons. To build this, the huge workforce first built a hill, then built the overpass on it, and then simply removed the hill leaving the overpass suspended in position.

Given the sheer scale of the Temple buildings and their stones, it would be entirely natural for one of Jesus' disciples to remark in awed tones about what he was seeing. There was simply nothing like this in Galilee - or anywhere else for that matter. By contrast, Jerusalem hosted a Temple complex of a magnitude that was without equal in the entire world. Little wonder that it was visible for miles around and required its own police force. In size and scale it surpassed anything and everything else. Even in Rome, no temple was its equal. It was all a far cry from the Tabernacle erected by Moses in the wilderness and the anointed pillar erected by Jacob at Bethel and yet it stood in exact and direct continuity with both of them. Bigger by far, it was still the gate of heaven, the place of sacrifice and atonement and the centre of the world. Like them, it was God's house; the place of his abiding presence to which pilgrims ascended singing songs of praise, in accordance with God's holy Law.

The Temple of His Body

How on earth could Jesus claim to *be* this; let alone *rebuild* it? It must have sounded like a bizarre and ridiculous claim: a ludicrous conceit or the wild ranting of a madman. And whilst John frequently uses misunderstanding of Jesus by his questioners as a vehicle for deeper elaboration of his points, it is not difficult to see how a claim to rebuild the Temple in three days would have completely perplexed everyone in earshot on that fateful day in the Court of the Gentiles. "Destroy this temple, and in three days I will raise it up" says Jesus, whip in hand, tables overturned, money scattered, animals driven out. Little wonder that the response of 'the Jews' to Jesus' claim is one of anger and incredulity: "It has taken forty-six years to build this Temple, and will you raise it up in three days?" (John 2: 19-20).

How likely is it, then, that Jesus made such a claim? And, if he did, how likely is it that John has reproduced his words accurately? At the very least we need to consider the possibility that he was either very misheard or that the claim was composed – by John or by others – retrospectively and in the light of the events that occurred at the end of Jesus' life when the belief began to circulate that he had been 'rebuilt' after his crucifixion. In support of the view that he made some kind of claim *during his life* about destruction of the Temple, an interval of three days, and some kind of rebuilding, is the fact that variants upon it occur in Matthew and Mark. In Matthew for example, we read that at Jesus' trial the chief priests and the 'whole council' were looking for 'false testimony' against him so that they could put him to death. Matthew says that they found none, despite the coming forward of many false witnesses. Finally two come forward with the claim that Jesus said "I am able to destroy the temple of God, and to rebuild it in three days." (Matthew 27: 59-61). This is quite similar to Mark's rendering of the wording of 'some' who 'bore false witness against him, saying "We heard him say, "I will destroy this temple that is made with hands, and in three days I will build another, not made with hands."" (Mark 14: 57-8).

Lending support to the fact that he said *something* by the end of his life about destroying and rebuilding the Temple in three days is the fact that later, after his trial and during his crucifixion, the 'in three days' phrase recurs again in Matthew and Mark. Matthew tells us that 'those who passed by derided him, wagging their heads and saying, "You who would destroy the temple and rebuild it in three days, save yourself! If you are the Son of God, come down from the cross"' (Matthew 27: 40). Mark tells us something very similar, that those passing by shook their heads, saying: "Aha! You who would destroy the temple and rebuild it in three days, save yourself and come down from the cross!" (Mark 15:

29-30). There is even what might be described as a 'veiled allusion' to some such claim by Luke in Acts 6: 13-14, where 'false witnesses' against Stephen claim before 'the council' that "This man never ceases to speak words against this holy place and the law, for we have heard him say that this Jesus of Nazareth will destroy this place and will change the customs that Moses delivered to us."

There is consistent evidence, then, that Jesus made some kind of claim during his lifetime involving the destruction and rebuilding of the Temple after three days and that the claim provided the basis for accusations at his trial and led in part to the mockery he received during his execution. The continual reiteration of the phrase 'in three days', in particular, lends support to the view that he said some such thing, that it had become common knowledge by the time of his death, and that it was connected with the Temple's destruction and rebuilding. Multiple attestation of consistent and linked elements of such a claim by Matthew, Mark and John – and perhaps in Acts too, if the reference at Stephen's trial is to the incident involving Jesus' claim - make it very likely that it is ultimately traceable to Jesus himself, in some form. The fact that he made the original claim – whatever the exact wording – in a packed public place during a major festival reinforces the possibility that it was overheard by many and later passed on: perhaps in various forms. Putting all of this together, it becomes potentially one of the best attested to of any of the claims that Jesus made during his earthly life.

An Authentic Construction

But what of the distinct language of the claim as recorded by John? Is it to be preferred, for example, to the words of his accusers in Matthew and/or Mark, or is what *they* say actually a closer rendering of what Jesus said in the Temple precincts? The actual grammatical construction of Jesus' challenge as reported by John to "Destroy this temple, and in three days I will raise it up" is an odd one but what is commonly accepted is that it is what is known as a conditional protasis, where the distinctive sense is one of 'if' and 'then', as in "*If* you believed Moses [*then*] you would believe me..." with the 'if' constituting the protasis and the 'then' constituting what is known as the apodosis. Many different relationships can exist between protasis and apodosis, but the crucial point is that for many scholars this distinct construction brings us close to an underlying semitic original: in other words, to the language Jesus spoke and to the kind of thing he would have said when he actually said it, *in the way that he would have said it.*

To be sure, Jesus' utterance in the Temple as recorded in John's gospel is a slightly *odd* sort of conditional protasis. For example, these sorts of sentences usually contain the Greek word 'ei', meaning 'if': a word not found in John 2:19. This being said, it is a highly unusual declaration anyway, and it is delivered in the form, almost, of a challenge or a reference to some kind of future eventuality. Thus, it might easily and equivalently be rendered: "*If* you destroy this temple, *then* in three days I will raise it up". In other words, as a conditional protasis, despite the absence of the 'ei'.

Given that such phrasing brings us close to an underlying original, some scholars have argued that what we have in John's gospel is the most primitive – as in 'authentic' – form of any of the gospels' declarations concerning the destruction of the Temple and Jesus' raising it up again. So not only does it look highly likely that Jesus said something about the Temple being destroyed and raised up again after three days, it also looks likely that John preserves the most accurate rendering of what Jesus *actually* said. And this, in turn, raises the intriguing possibility that his words on that day were accurately heard and recalled by somebody who was also in the Temple precincts; somebody who saw the commotion that Jesus caused and heard what was said in its aftermath.

'Zeal For Your House Will Consume Me!'

The evidence, then, is very strong that Jesus did and said what John says he did and said. Even a sceptical reader might well concede that the acts and the utterance are very well attested to and that the author of John's gospel might therefore have actually been there when the events unfolded: seeing and hearing everything. But we cannot end this chapter without considering *why* Jesus did what he did. What enraged him so on that day?

There are numerous possible answers to this question and several can be dismissed at the outset. If Jesus was trying to mount an actual assault on the Temple – to physically destroy it, in other words – he would have needed more than a whip and twelve disciples. In fact, he would have needed a considerable army and would have been forced to reckon with not just the anger of the Temple authorities but also with the wrath of the Temple guards, whose job it was to maintain order and who would have been out in force during Passover. And over and above these would have been the Romans, themselves out in force during this festival and alert to the slightest hint of Jewish insurrection: then and always.

Not an assault, then. What else? It is possible that Jesus was simply being downright unreasonable, yet this possibility also collapses on closer analysis. It is a fact that during Passover the pilgrims' money needed to be changed. Required to pay the Temple Tax and coming from all over the Roman Empire and beyond, they would have bought all kinds of different coins with them. But they could not pay the Temple Tax with any coin that bore the image of a pagan god or king. So the money changers would have been on hand to change their money into approved coinage: Tyrian shekels. And, of course, then as now, money changers would require a fee for providing this service. This was not unreasonable and everybody including Jesus would have known that such a system needed to be in place in order for the Temple to operate.

Moreover, the sacrifices that the pilgrims were required to present according to the Mosaic law had to be checked for blemishes by the priests. If an animal intended for sacrifice failed the test, it could not be offered. Imagine struggling for hundreds of miles with a sacrifice, only to find that it was blemished in ways that made it unacceptable as a Temple offering. Much better, therefore, to travel unencumbered and to buy an approved offering on your arrival at the Temple. Hence the presence of sellers of animals and birds in the Temple precincts. Again, it seems highly unlikely that Jesus would have been surprised to find such an arrangement in place or would have been unaware that such a system was necessary.

It is also unlikely that Jesus' Galilean background would set him in any way in opposition to the Temple. It has been suggested, for example, that the reverence for the Temple that was very much in evidence in Jerusalem would have been missing in Galilee, where a simpler and less elaborate Judaism would have prevailed. But yet again this suggestion can be countered. Recent archaeological evidence has shown that there was much reverence for the Temple in Galilee and elsewhere. Indeed, there is a strong sense in which such distant places cherished their connection to the Holy City and its Temple. To give one example: clay oil lamps found at Yodefat in Galilee, some 94 miles north of Jerusalem, have been shown to have been brought from Jerusalem, whereas all other artefacts such as cooking pots, storage jars and jugs have been shown to be of local origin. This suggests that their flame was seen in some sense as an 'extension' of the Temple's holiness and light, 'carried' to the provinces by lamps which were brought there by returning pilgrims. More than mere 'souvenirs', these lamps extended the holiness of the Temple into Galilee, an extension that would hardly have been seen as desirous if the Temple itself was not cherished there.

Perhaps, then, Jesus' action in the Temple should be seen as a rejection of the Temple itself. Indeed, this has been a historically popular point of view and is still widely held. According to this position, the incident shows Jesus rejecting the Jewish faith into which he was born; or, at least, key aspects of it to do with sacrifice and everything else associated with the Temple. The problem here is that this goes against everything else that we know about him. He was called 'rabbi' both by his friends and by his enemies. He wore tassels on his garment, as evidenced by the healing of the woman with the haemorrhage as recorded in Matthew, Mark and Luke (Matthew 9: 18-26; Mark 5: 21-43; Luke 8: 40-56). He attended the synagogue on the Sabbath. He loved the Jewish law, and as far as we can tell he kept it. He was presented at the Temple by his parents and visited it – John tells us – several times during his life. John also tells us that he taught there. Perhaps he even sacrificed there. And after his death the early Jerusalem Christian community continued to gather there, as is clear from Acts. This all suggests that Jesus was deeply devoted to his Jewish faith, a devotion that extended to those elements of it connected to the Temple and which was carried on by the earliest Christians.

"...But You Have Made It a Den of Robbers"

One final possibility presents itself. It is that Jesus' actions were a deliberate attempt on his part to recall to the minds of his hearers and witnesses the words and actions of Israel's earlier prophets, and that he intended those who saw and heard him to make the connection. His words as recorded in Matthew 21:13 and similarly recorded by Mark and Luke – "It is written, 'My house shall be called a house of prayer', but you make it a den of robbers'" – are not found in John's gospel, but it is very possible that Jesus spoke them or something very like them and that they, too, were heard in the midst of what we have already seen was a very crowded place. After all, it would be unlikely that he only said one short thing or made one brief declaration either during his actions or afterwards, when he was called on to justify what he had done.

The 'den of robbers' quote comes from Jeremiah 7:11, where the full quote reads: "'Has this house, which is called by my name, become a den of robbers in your eyes? Behold, I myself have seen it", declares the LORD'. The wider context for this verse is Jeremiah's claim that the Temple that existed during his time would be destroyed: which, of course, it was by the Babylonians and in circumstances already described at the beginning of this chapter. Might it have been the case that Jesus meant his actions and his words to be understood as a prophecy of the destruction of the Temple that existed during *his* life? This remains as a very likely possibility, but even if it is accepted it does not explain Jesus' anger and the reasons for this: it merely provides a context and commentary on what he said and did. Can we, then, go deeper still?

Consuming the Goods of the Poor

One thing has become clear as a result of the increased scholarly attention that Herod's Temple has drawn in recent years: by Jesus' time it had become associated with very corrupt practices and these were very widely known. Writings from this time talk of greed and avarice and there are suggestions that pilgrims were even being charged an entrance fee in order to gain admission. Shockingly, some of the more junior priests were even driven to starvation by the actions of the High Priest and during the dynasty of Annas, for example, there was often violent extortion and many priests suffered greatly. By contrast, the High Priestly family lived very well; relying on bribery of the Romans to keep their position which made them almost untouchable and which also allowed them to do virtually what they liked. There is evidence that they amassed great wealth during the period and it is clear from excavated ruins that many of the ruling priests of the period had lavish houses and ornate tombs.

These and other troubling practices are confirmed by the contemporary historian Josephus and may explain why the group who removed themselves to Qumran – the so-called 'Dead Sea Covenanters' who produced the Dead Sea Scrolls – were operating as a sort of substitute, 'emergency', Temple, in the middle of the Dead Sea desert. Appalled by what they saw and heard, they had effectively set themselves up as another, purer, House of God, and many of their writings reflect this. The Talmud also reinforces a view of the High Priesthood at this time as decadent, mercenary and corrupt, declaring that 'They loved money and hated each other.' Money that flowed into the Temple – partly through the Temple Tax – was used for high interest loans that often led to poor landowners losing their lands. And there was also the practice of *qorban*, in which giving to the Temple even overrode care for one's parents: a practice which Jesus condemned, but one which once again could be taken advantage of by the ruling priesthood. And these disturbing states of affairs were widely known. One text dated to the period, the Testament of Moses, writes of these priests of the ruling priesthood that:

'They consume the goods of the [poor], saying their acts are according to justice, [while in fact they are simply] exterminators, deceitfully seeking to conceal themselves so that they will not be known as completely godless...They, with hand and mind, touch impure things, yet their mouths will speak enormous things, and they will even say, "Do not touch me, lest you pollute me in the position I occupy"' (*T. Mos.* 7: 6-10)

Taken together, this evidence is disturbing and uncomfortable and it paints a very unhappy picture. Read at face value it appears to show that the Temple and some of its operations might well have equated to the 'den of robbers' description that Jesus used as he staged his deliberately evocative protest: one designed to recall to mind what had happened in earlier times when disastrous consequences for the Temple followed times of greed and corruption on the part of those whose very task it should have been to keep God's house pure.

"It Has Taken Forty-Six Years to Build This Temple"

So why, then, *does* John omit any reference to the 'den of robbers' line that the other gospel writers include? The omission is doubly strange if we suppose, as suggested earlier in this chapter, that the writer of John's gospel was actually present in the Temple Courts when Jesus staged his protest and was therefore in a good position to have heard everything that was said. One possibility is that John alone amongst the gospel writers sees a meaning and significance to Jesus' words and actions that he is particularly anxious to emphasise and that he wants nothing to obscure or detract from this; particularly in view of the fact that Jesus' words as he reproduces them seem so enigmatic and strange. They certainly seem that way to his accusers, whose retort that "It has taken forty-six years to build this temple, and will you raise it up in three days?" suggests that they do not understand what Jesus means at all.

By this early point in his gospel, however, *we* the readers have begun to understand. In fact, Jesus' words in the Temple embody a distinct claim that we have heard at least twice before and we are still only at the gospel's second chapter. Indeed, the question of why Jesus did what he did on the day that he 'cleansed' the Temple may be secondary. The most important point to grasp is the fact that Jesus is again making an explicit claim to *be* the Temple. John has already prepared the reader for this in his equating of Jesus with the Tabernacle in his Prologue and in his portrayal of Jesus as the one claiming to be he upon whom angels will ascend and descend in his description of the calling of the earliest disciples at the end of that chapter. Now the claim is being made in an even more emphatic way and the reader made even more vividly aware of what is being asserted. For by the end of the second chapter of John's gospel the claim has been rooted in a very public assertion accompanying a very dramatic action in the very place where its meaning might be expected to be most fully grasped by those with 'ears to hear'. Jesus' "Destroy this Temple and in three days I will raise it up again" may indeed include the sense of "Destroy my body..." but it is clear both from the context and from what has gone before in his gospel that John means much more than this. Jesus *is* the Temple, he is telling us, but in ways that his gospel has yet to fully convey.

In fact, John's locating of the incident in the Temple at the beginning of his gospel – and not, as with the other gospel writers, at the end - reinforces the view that, for him, it contains something of supreme importance for the understanding of the rest of his narrative which requires it to be there almost at the very outset. It is, in fact, tempting to view his recounting of the incident as a kind of 'manifesto' setting out once again what he will later make more explicit still: the startling claim that Jesus *is* in some sense the Temple, with all of the enormous consequences and implications that this fact brings with it. Unsurprisingly, John has very much more to say about Jesus as the Temple. Next time, however, the setting for this remarkable claim will be a very different one from that of the Temple in Jerusalem.

Chapter Four: Dead Water, Living Water

A woman from Samaria came to draw water. Jesus said to her, "Give me a drink." (For his disciples had gone away into the city to buy food.) The Samaritan woman said to him, "How is it that you, a Jew, ask for a drink from me, a woman of Samaria?" (For Jews have no dealings with Samaritans.) Jesus answered her, "If you knew the gift of God, and who it is that is saying to you, 'Give me a drink', you would have asked him, and he would have given you living water." The woman said to him, "Sir, you have nothing to draw water with, and the well is deep. Where do you get that living water? Are you greater than our father Jacob? He gave us this well and drank from it himself, as did his sons and his livestock." Jesus said to her, "Everyone who drinks of this water will be thirsty again, but whoever drinks of the water that I will give him will never be thirsty again. The water that I will give him will become in him a spring of water welling up to eternal life."

John 4: 7-14

Sea of Death

Located between Israel and Jordan, about 15 miles east of Jerusalem, is the Dead Sea. It gets its name because nothing can live in it, with the exception of some varieties of algae and a strain of bacteria called *halapholis* which, one suspects, could live just about anywhere. Massively saltier than the world's living oceans, it has a sea bed curiously devoid of life and fish that swim into its waters are killed instantly. It is the world's deepest hypersaline lake.

At its deepest the Dead Sea is over 700 metres below sea level. The deeper it goes the saltier it gets and below 90 metres the water is

51

effectively saturated with salt and it is this salt toxicity that is so fatal to virtually all life. So why is it so salty? If the Dead Sea is compared with a living sea within the region – such as the Sea of Galilee – the answer becomes obvious. The Sea of Galilee teems with life and in the gospels – including John's gospel – we read about it over and over again. Before they became his followers, for example, Jesus' disciples used to fish in it and sometimes the catches were impressive: on occasion miraculously so. In contrast to the Dead Sea, the Sea of Galilee is a *living* sea. It lives because the River Jordan enters it at its North and exits it at its South. So water flows into and through it and out of it – water in, water out. By contrast, the Dead Sea has water flowing in but *not* out. It is what is known as a 'closed basin'. So why does it not continually flood? The answer to this is found in the hot climate of the region. The area of the Dead Sea is so hot that water evaporates rapidly, ensuring that it *never* floods. But this leaves behind salt. So the more it evaporates, the saltier it gets. And the saltier it gets, the deader it stays. And it never dries up because the River Jordan keeps feeding it with water.

It is not the Dead Sea's 'fault' that it is dead. In the Book of Ezekiel, in Chapter 47 verse 9, we read: 'everything will live where the river goes.' But it stops at the Dead Sea and everything dies. The implications of this are interesting, and the Dead Sea has sometimes been used as a metaphor or parable for our human lives. For we, too, seem designed to both receive and give. So when everything flows - in and out - everything lives. But if we receive and do not give, we, in a sense, die: like the Dead Sea. And this isn't necessarily about physical or financial well-being. It could be gifts, talents, abilities, anything. The rule seems to be: let in and let out. It certainly seems to be a Biblical principle, and this was what all good rabbis knew they must do. As Paul wrote to the Corinthians: 'For I delivered to you as of first importance what I also received: that Christ died for our sins...' (1 Corinthians 15: 3). In other words: 'what I gave to you I, in turn, received. I gave out what I also took in.'

But the Bible teaches something else about the Dead Sea as well, and the implications of this are profound. For in the Book of Ezekiel we read that the Dead Sea will not always be dead. One day it will live. Given its present state of salt saturation and consequent toxicity, this sounds like a remarkable – even unbelievable - claim. But Ezekiel the prophet writes that this is what he saw in one of his many strange visions. He tells too of how it will come about. And it is a story that provides much of the background, context and explanation for a vital episode in the Gospel of John.

Water from the Threshold

Ezekiel is something of an enigma. The third of the Major Prophets after Isaiah and Jeremiah, he was born into a priestly family in approximately 623 BCE and the Old Testament book that bears his name is remarkable for the series of visions, prophesies and revelations that it contains, centred in large part around the Temple, its destruction, and its restoration. We are back in time from Herod's day. His glorious Temple and its precincts – including the one in which Jesus caused such a commotion on that fateful Passover - lie many centuries in the future. The Book of Ezekiel begins with the prophet amongst the exiles driven from the land of Israel by the Babylonians and this locates it within the history of Israel very precisely, in circumstances we have already examined. Chapter ten of the Book of Ezekiel sets out a vision of God leaving this Temple prior to its destruction because of the dreadful practices that have been going on there and later we read in Ezekiel chapter 16 that God has pronounced judgement on Israel because she has been a "harlot bride". Hence the destruction of both Jerusalem and the Temple which Ezekiel sees from afar. But later still in that chapter it is made clear by God that the people of Israel will return from their exile, and later still that He will "restore the fortunes of Jacob" and "have mercy on the whole house of Israel", that another Temple will replace the previous one, and that God's presence will return to it. No less than seven of the last eight chapters of the Book of Ezekiel describe the dimensions and characteristics of this restored Temple, together with some of the remarkable events that will follow its restoration.

Overall, it has been calculated from evidence internal to the Book of Ezekiel that the prophet was 25 when he went into exile, 30 when he received his prophetic call, and 52 when he received his final vision of the new Temple. The description of the new Temple that commences in chapter 40 is detailed and precise and it includes rules for the priests. The returning glory of the Lord is described in chapter 43. But it is chapter 47 that is most important here. In a vivid passage filled with striking imagery, Ezekiel is given a vision of an apparently future time when water will flow out of this new Temple, "issuing from below the threshold...towards the east..." Flowing "south of the altar", it runs eastwards. First it is ankle-deep, then knee-deep, then waist-deep, and finally Ezekiel writes that "I could not pass through, for the water had risen. It was deep enough to swim in, a river that could not be passed through." Incredibly, however, verse eight brings yet another development within an already remarkable and unexpected passage. Here, Ezekiel learns that:

> "'This water flows towards the eastern region and goes into the Arabah, and enters the Dead Sea; when the water flows into the sea, the water will become fresh. And wherever the river goes, every living creature that swarms will live, and there will be very many fish. For this water goes there, that the waters of the sea may become fresh; so everything will live where the river goes. Fishermen will stand beside the sea...But its swamps and marshes will not become fresh; they are to be left for salt. And on the banks, on both sides of the river, there will grow all kinds of trees for food. Their leaves will not wither, nor their fruit fail, but they will bear fresh fruit every month, because the water for them flows from the sanctuary. Their fruit will be for food, and their leaves for healing'" (Ezekiel 47: 8-12).

Water flowing from the Temple's innermost parts: from its very sanctuary! *Living* water, that brings life where it flows and which gushes eastwards and downwards into the Dead Sea, making it teem, as the LORD tells Ezekiel, with "many fish" and "every living creature that swarms". It is a 'twist' in an already remarkable narrative that surely no reader could have anticipated. Previously, in a very famous passage, Ezekiel has described a valley of dry bones bought to life (Ezekiel 37: 1-14). But here, in a lesser-known sequence, it is a dead sea – *the* Dead Sea - that lives. It is a dramatic scenario, and it provides what is virtually the climax of a fascinating and mysterious book. It is certainly the climactic moment in a narrative that bears prophetic witness to a landscape transformed by water that flows from a newly-restored Temple, and which brings both food and healing wherever it goes.

Symbols and Reality

Of course, the Book of Ezekiel is full of vivid images, and many of the 'vision sequences' it contains are just that: visions. To take them literally would be to miss the point. In the famous 'Valley of Dry Bones' episode in chapter 37, for example, Ezekiel is shown a dramatic vision sequence in which dead bones come back to life, gaining sinews, flesh, skin, and finally breath. The image is a prophecy of Israel's restoration and return to the land from which she has been exiled. She will 'come back from the dead', says God, in effect, to Ezekiel. Not literally, but symbolically, with the actual return to the land pictured in symbolic form as being akin to the rising of the people from the dust of death. It would be a somewhat inconsistent thing, therefore, to treat Ezekiel's other 'vision sequences' as literal rather than symbolic truths: the Dead Sea story included. This is not, however, the really important thing when we consider how the story is recalled to mind in chapter four of John's gospel. Rather, in the story of Jesus and the Samaritan woman, the important thing is the light it sheds on Jesus' identity and the implications of this for the reader's developing understanding of who he was and is.

A Meeting at Midday

Jesus' well-known meeting with Nicodemus in chapter three of John's gospel and his meeting with a Samaritan woman in chapter four provide an interesting pair of stories with a shared structure. But there is one marked contrast. Nicodemus comes to Jesus 'by night', but the encounter with the Samaritan woman occurs by day: in the baking heat of the middle of the day, at 'about the sixth hour.' 'Jesus', says John, 'had to pass through Samaria' *en route* from Judea to Galilee and he and the disciples came to a town called Sychar 'near the plot of ground Jacob had given to his son Joseph' (John 4: 5). A tremendous amount is being conveyed in these few brief words. Today, just as it did at the time of Jesus, Jacob's well stands in the shadow of Mount Gerizim, and it was on this mountain that the Samaritans believed God had commanded the Temple to be built. This explains the woman's 'history lesson' to Jesus in verse 20: "Our fathers worshipped on this mountain, but you say that in Jerusalem is the place where people ought to worship." This is a pivotal moment in this strange encounter. Where should the Temple *really* be? As we have seen, for Jews it was in Jerusalem. But Samaritans believed something very different. The Samaritan bible differed in some key respects from the Jewish one, lacking some prophetic books and differing in other significant ways also and in it there was, in effect, a commandment in addition to the others received by Moses which, echoing Deuteronomy 27: 2-7, made clear – to the Samaritans - that there should be an altar on Mount Gerizim of unhewn stones where sacrifices should be made. Crucial for them were instructions that made this location very clear, together with instructions concerning how the altar was to be made, what could and could not be used in its construction, how its stones should be plastered, what offerings were to be made on it and what should be written on it.

This disagreement over where the 'Real Temple' should actually be was one of the crucial things that contributed to the deep division between Jews and Samaritans at the time of Jesus and it is another crucial key for the understanding of John's story of Jesus and the Samaritan woman. Indeed, by Jesus' time, Jews effectively saw the world as being split into three peoples: Jews, Gentiles, and Samaritans. They cursed Samaritans in the synagogues. They said that Samaritan bread was like pig flesh. The fact that when they wanted to insult Jesus they called him, on occasion, a Samaritan is revealing inasmuch as it shows the deeply ingrained hostility towards Samaritans that existed during Jesus' day. Samaritans were, in effect, viewed as an idolatrous people, hated by God, and with no hope for salvation. But towering above all of this was a fundamental disagreement about where the Temple should be. Indeed, the hostility between Jews and Samaritans was reciprocal, and Samaritans had desecrated the Jerusalem Temple during Passover in 9 CE, thus continuing and perpetuating many centuries of enmity. It is against this backdrop and in the shadow of Mount Gerizim that John's tale of a remarkable encounter unfolds.

"Give Me a Drink"

We have already noted the difficulties that can be encountered in distinguishing symbolic and literal elements in some biblical episodes and the story of Jesus and the Samaritan woman gives another example of this. John tells us in verse 6 that 'it was about the sixth hour': one of many points in the gospel in which precise information suggestive of eyewitness testimony is conveyed. Whilst drawing water would normally be a communal activity, the Samaritan woman clearly shuns this, preferring to draw alone and at the hottest part of the day. She clearly has a bucket – you would bring your own – but Jesus apparently does not have one, and asks her, in effect, to use hers to draw some water for him. Unsurprisingly the woman is taken aback by this request, asking "How is it that you, a Jew, ask for a drink from me, a woman of Samaria?" And at this point we are shown a story-telling technique that John has already used – for example, in his description of Jesus' nocturnal 'encounter' with Nicodemus – and which he will use virtually throughout the remainder of his gospel. In essence, a series of declarations by Jesus are misunderstood by his hearers, allowing deeper and deeper description and clarification, before understanding finally dawns for them. And while Jesus' hearers typically misunderstand because they interpret his words on a physical, this-worldly, level, the reader is allowed to discern an unfolding *spiritual* truth as the encounter plays out. It is a characteristic way that John uses to bring out the meaning of Jesus' words, and he uses it to brilliant effect here.

"Where Do You Get That Living Water?"

Jesus ignores the woman's shock and surprise at his request by declaring "If you knew the gift of God, and who it is that is saying to you, "Give me a drink", you would have asked him, and he would have given you living water." The woman replies respectfully, but her words show that she has completely missed the point: "Sir, you have nothing to draw water with, and the well is deep. Where do you get that living water? Are you greater than our father Jacob? He gave us this well and drank from it himself, as did his sons and his livestock." Jesus ignores the history lesson (one which, however, allows John to fill his readers in on more of the underlying context of the encounter) and makes a second declaration: "Everyone who drinks of this water will be thirsty again, but whoever drinks of the water that I give him will never be thirsty again. The water that I will give him will become in him a spring of water welling up to eternal life." And once again the woman misunderstands: "Sir, give me this water, so that I will not be thirsty or have to come here to draw water."

So far it is interesting that whilst the woman responds to Jesus' words, John portrays Jesus as never directly responding to hers; preferring, instead, to focus on his words almost as a progressive series of revelations. There is, however, a pronounced 'shift' in verse sixteen, where Jesus suddenly and abruptly commands the woman to "Go, call your husband, and come here." This is unexpected: by the woman and reader alike. But she apparently understands what she is being asked to do and responds by saying that she, in fact, has no husband. And now Jesus' reply *is* direct: "You are right in saying, 'I have no husband'; for you have had five husbands, and the one you now have is not your husband. What you have said is true." Clearly impressed at this remarkable insight – how could Jesus possibly know this? – the woman declares that he is a prophet, and with this shows that understanding is, at last, beginning to stir. And maybe she is becoming more comfortable in the presence of this discerning stranger, because she even enters into a little 'inter-religious dialogue' concerning the Temple's location: "Our fathers worshipped on this mountain, but you say that in Jerusalem is the place people ought to worship." With this, John is again able to fill in a little more context and backdrop, and it is an important moment in the dialogue, because, opening up as she now is, the woman still misunderstands a point which he wants to make very clear. So Jesus responds to the woman's misunderstanding once more, in the most detailed way yet:

> "'Woman, believe me, the hour is coming when neither on this mountain nor in Jerusalem will you worship the Father. You

worship what you do not know; we worship what we know, for salvation is from the Jews. But the hour is coming, and is now here, when the true worshippers will worship the Father in spirit and truth, for the Father is seeking such people to worship him. God is spirit, and those who worship him must worship in spirit and truth'" (John 4: 21-24).

Prior to this the woman had arrived at the conclusion that this stranger was a prophet, but in the light of these words her next assertion reveals that she has begun to think of him as something – or somebody – much greater. Maybe she thinks out loud when she says: "I know that Messiah (called Christ) is coming. When he comes, he will explain everything to us." But there can be no more misunderstanding in the light of what follows. John tells us, simply, that Jesus says to her: "I who speak to you am he." With this, the dialogue reaches its climax. It is just as if Jesus had said: "I am the Messiah." After such a stunning revelation, what more could possibly be said?

And indeed, so much has happened in this brief encounter that anything that comes after is *bound* to be an anti-climax. The disciples return. The woman leaves her water jar at the well – physical water now forgotten - and goes back into town; calling her people, in effect, to go out to meet this incredible man. Later we learn that many Samaritans from that same town come to believe in Jesus and ask him to stay with them, which he does for two days, before resuming his journey to Galilee (John 4: 27-43).

"I Who Speak To You Am He"

"I who speak to you am he". It is a straightforward but startling claim to be the Messiah: a clear declaration from Jesus as to his identity and it is crucial for a full understanding of this story. Yet there is more here even than this, for by the time of Jesus the belief had grown up that the Messiah would be the one who would do various wonderful things, and one of these would be the rebuilding of the Temple. Various texts were being read like this: texts that would be familiar to Jesus and those Jews – and perhaps others - with whom he interacted. Zechariah 6: 12-13, for example, was being widely interpreted in exactly this way. The text reads: "'And say to him, 'Thus says the LORD of hosts: "Behold the man whose name is the Branch: for he shall branch out from his place, and he shall build the temple of the Lord and shall bear royal honour, and shall sit and rule on his throne."'" By the first century CE, the Targums - Aramaic commentaries and interpretations of the scriptures typically heard in synagogues - were customarily rendering 'Branch' in this passage as 'Messiah', turning it into a prophecy that the Messiah would be the one to rebuild the Temple. Other passages – found both inside and outside the Western canon of scripture – were being interpreted in similar ways, including 2 Samuel 7: 13: "When your days are fulfilled and you lie down with your ancestors, I will raise up your offspring after you, who will come forth from your body, and I will establish his kingdom. He shall build a house for my name, and I will establish the throne of his kingdom forever." As with the Zechariah text, this text too was being understood by the time of Jesus as a reference to what the Messiah would do, once again underlining the widespread expectation that the Messiah would in some sense be one who rebuilt the Temple.

"Are You the Christ?"

In fact, this belief during Jesus' day that the Messiah would be the one who would build a new 'Messianic' Temple in place of the old one helps to explain another incident – found in both Matthew and Mark – that would otherwise be rather puzzling. It will be recalled that at Jesus' trial as recorded in both gospels there are various 'false witnesses' who make accusations about Jesus' words in the Temple regarding its destruction and rebuilding. Mark, for example, has a 'witness' saying: "We heard him say, 'I will destroy this temple that is made with hands, and in three days I will build another, not made with hands." The High Priest then says to Jesus: "Have you no answer to make? What is it that these men testify against you?" but, as Mark records, Jesus makes no response. The implication and import of their accusations is not lost on the High Priest, however, who fills the silence with another question: "Are you the Christ [i.e the Messiah], the son of the Blessed?" (Mark 14: 57-61). He knows full well that any claim to destroy and rebuild the Temple is an automatic claim to be the

Messiah, and this explains what would otherwise be an inexplicable 'fresh tack' in the questioning, when it is in fact no such thing. Understood in the light of what it was expected that the Messiah would do, it is simply a logical corollary of the accusation that the witnesses have brought before him and the council. The Messiah will rebuild the Temple; *ergo* if this man is claiming to do the latter he must be the former.

So at the climax of Jesus' dialogue with the Woman of Samaria as recorded by John, an assertion is made that would be very revealing to anyone sharing or understanding what first-century Jews thought the Messiah would do: including the writer of the gospel and any readership with an awareness of first-century Messianic expectation. In claiming to be the Messiah, Jesus must be claiming to rebuild the Temple too. And, of course, the reader has already been learning in this gospel that Jesus *is* the Temple, that he *will* rebuild it, and that it will be and is nothing less than his body. The episode in chapter two, and in particular Jesus' invitation to "Destroy this temple, and in three days I will raise it up!" – together with John's own commentary on it - has made all of this very clear, although as we have seen, the identification of Jesus with the Temple has been made by John from the beginning. And this developing identification, in turn, now throws fresh light on the whole passage at Jacob's well and particularly those aspects of it to do with where the Temple is. As already noted, the Samaritan woman knows very well that Jews and Samaritans have their differences, and that one of these relates to the Temple's location. As we have seen, Jesus introduces a 'twist' into this debate by asserting, in effect, that the Temple is neither where Jews think it is nor where Samaritans think it is. For him, recall, "[T]he hour is coming when neither on this mountain nor in Jerusalem will you worship the Father." This is a shocking claim, but Jesus follows it up with the equally remarkable assertion that "[T]he hour is coming, *and is now here*, when the true worshippers will worship the Father in spirit and truth, for the Father is seeking such people to worship him" (Emphasis mine). What could the meaning of this be?

At this point it is crucial to notice where, exactly, Jesus *is* when he is talking with the woman. John tells us in verse 6 that he is apparently sitting *beside* the well. Or does he? The greek word for 'beside' is actually *para*. But it is not the word that John uses. He uses *epi*, which means 'on'. So, according to John, Jesus sits not beside but *on* Jacob's well. It will be his later translators - and they are virtually unanimous in rendering *epi* incorrectly as 'beside' – who misunderstand. Yet there is nothing terribly odd about Jesus sitting on the well, given that wells typically had crude covers on them: usually of wood or stone. In fact, it is more probable that Jesus would sit *on* rather than *beside* the well, given that the actual covered well would be the only seat. It is the more likely historical and geographical scenario.

But is this *all* that there is to it? Given what John has already told us in his gospel, and what he is telling us in this episode, it is tempting once again to look for the deeper meaning under the surface of the text: particularly in the light of John's developing portrayal of Jesus as the Temple. And, sure enough, a deeper truth *is* revealed when we read his gospel in this way. To understand this, however, we need to think about a kind of Jewish theological writing known as *Midrash*.

Primordial Waters

Midrash is a form or type of historical rabbinic literature containing teachings and commentaries of rabbis over several centuries. Thus, *midrashim* are typically composed of interpretations of scriptures and may contain stories, discussions, and teachings: often designed to answer questions. The earliest of these, whilst dating from the century after Jesus, typically contain earlier teachings and traditions and are sometimes used by scholars to reconstruct earlier forms of Jewish life and thought. One such text - *Midrash Tanhuma* - reveals a very interesting view of the Holy Land as being composed of what might be likened to a series of concentric circles. It states:

'Just as the navel is found at the centre of a human being, so the land of Israel is found at the centre of the world. Jerusalem is at the centre of the land of Israel, and the temple is at the centre of Jerusalem, the Holy of Holies is at the centre of the temple, the Ark is at the centre of the Holy of Holies, and the Foundation Stone is in front of the Ark, which spot is the foundation of the world' (*Midrash Tanhuma* 10).

Dating *Midrash Tanhuma* is difficult, but it is believed that whilst it was edited as late as the ninth century it contains material considerably – probably many centuries - older, and it consists of interpretations and commentaries on a range of issues to do with the first five books of the Hebrew Bible. In the passage quoted above, we have an image of the Temple as navel, or *omphalos*, and as being located on what is referred to as the 'Foundation Stone', which in turn appears to be connected to the foundation of the entire world. Whilst this sounds very odd it is in fact a teaching that was widespread in the ancient world, with the notion of a 'Foundation Stone' reflecting other traditions found elsewhere – such as in Egypt - which teach that one particular part of the Earth was the point from which the rest of creation proceeded. Some Jewish traditions actually connected this 'primordial stone', or rock, to the one upon which Jacob slept when he dreamed his dream of the ladder connecting heaven and earth, but what is important to note here is that other traditions taught that under the Foundation Stone were the chaotic, primordial waters, and that the Temple actually 'capped' these, thus keeping them in place under a deep fissure in the ground. Sometimes, this fissure was said to be the source of the waters referred to in Genesis 2: 10. Still other traditions contained the belief that after the flood it was the rock of Noah's altar that sealed up the departed flood waters, and these linked this altar with the Foundation Stone in the Temple's Holy of Holies. Thus, however variously expressed, a shared belief was that waters would actually flow from under the Temple if it were not for the fact that the Temple rested upon them and thus kept them in place by, in effect, 'capping' them. And again, this is reflected in other ancient traditions, with one old Neo-Sumerian Temple hymn containing the line: 'Temple, at its top a mountain, at its bottom a spring.' It is also reflected in Ezekiel's vision of a Temple from which life-giving water has once again begun to flow.

So when Jesus claims to be the source of life-giving water, the like of which has never flowed, the historical and theological weight of this assertion is clear and the implications profound. Here is the Temple which, like that of Ezekiel's vision, is one from which life-giving waters will flow, so that everything will live where the river goes. The Samaritan woman may confuse this end-of-time water with physical water but, like so often in John, the reader knows more than the character. And with this knowing comes a tide of implications which is irresistible.

Flowing From the Sanctuary

John draws together a complex cluster of associations in his description of Jesus' encounter with the Woman of Samaria and by the time we have come to its end it is as if we have travelled along yet another tributary and have been returned once again to the ongoing flow of his gospel: one which is carrying us ever further and deeper into our recognition of who John is showing Jesus to be. Where is the Temple? John shows us in his account of the meeting of Jesus with the Woman of Samaria that it is neither in Jerusalem nor on Mount Gerizim. It is, in fact, a *person*: one greater even than Jacob and sitting atop – and not beside - Jacob's well. Whilst Jacob may have recognised the House of God – in dramatic circumstances that we have already explored – Jesus, as Messiah, is destined to rebuild it. In fact, this gospel is revealing him to be both Temple-builder *and* Temple. For, as the source of living waters, he is that to which Ezekiel's vision points: not a physical structure measured in cubits with a specific location but one from whom, nonetheless, life-giving waters will flow. He promises that a time is coming and is already here when the result of all this will be worship not in a contested location but in another 'dimension' altogether: one of spirit and truth. And his declaration of all of this, sitting upon a fissure from which real water flows, is a brilliant narrative touch by an author whose story drips with scarcely veiled irony and brilliant symbolic expression. Asking for physical water, Jesus is portrayed as the source of water of a much more important kind. Seated upon – *epi* - Jacob's well, he 'caps' it, as it was believed the Temple did with the primordial waters. But Jesus is greater, even than this. He offers a different kind of water; one which will never leave the drinker thirsty again. If only the woman knew who he was she would ask him for it! But the reader knows, thanks to the deftness and artistry of the author, and by the end of the episode the implications of this knowledge have become even clearer. Jesus, says John, is the Temple from whom life-giving waters flow: the one to whom Ezekiel's narrative points; one even greater than Jacob. He is the Foundation stone, the threshold, the source, and his is the water. It seems that nothing more can be said. What could possibly top this? But John has barely started, and Jesus as the Temple from which living and life-giving waters flow is a theme to which he will return in ever more remarkable and revealing ways.

Chapter Four: Dead Water, Living Water

Chapter Five: Tabernacles and Dedication

On the last day of the feast, the great day, Jesus stood up and cried out, "If anyone thirsts, let him come to me and drink. Whoever believes in me, as the Scripture has said, 'Out of his heart will flow rivers of living water.'" Now this he said about the Spirit, whom those who believed in him were to receive, for as yet the Spirit had not been given, because Jesus was not yet glorified.

John 7: 37-9

The Feast of Tabernacles

Few things mark the passing of time like seasons and festivals and whatever else might unexpectedly befall us during the course of a year, they never fail to arrive. And they are typically linked. Like all calendars, the Jewish calendar is marked by feasts and festivals, and many of them are related closely to the seasons in which they occur. The Feast of Tabernacles – or Succoth – is typical in this respect. Falling in late September and early October, it has many intertwined historical and theological roots, and it has as one of its features an aspect similar to Christianity's Harvest Festival. This was true in Jesus' day, just as it is in our own. With the harvests all in, it was a time for great rejoicing: so much so that it was sometimes just called 'the Feast', although the name 'Succoth' actually means 'Booths'. This word gives a vivid and accurate key to its roots within the history of Israel. We noted in chapter one how the journey through the desert after the exodus from Egypt was marked by transience and movement. A pillar of fire guided the people of Israel during their journey to the Promised Land. When it moved, they moved. When it stayed, they stayed. It was a nomadic existence, and even Israel's God dwelt in a tent.

Booths has been a constant reminder to Jews since that time of how they lived in their earliest days as a people, and the Festival has its scriptural roots in an injunction found in Leviticus chapter 23. Here the Torah enjoins Jewish people to celebrate the feast for seven days, with a first day and an eighth day devoted to "solemn rest". Key to what Succoth involves are the components of the celebration as decreed by the scriptures. So, Leviticus 23: 40 reads: "And you shall take on the first day the fruit of splendid trees, branches of palm trees and boughs of leafy trees and willows of the brook, and you shall rejoice before the Lord your God for seven days." And then we read in verse 42: "You shall dwell in booths for seven days. All native Israelites shall dwell in booths, that your generations may know that I made the people of Israel dwell in booths when I brought them out of the Land of Egypt: I am the LORD your God."

Water and Light

Throughout their history, Jewish people have celebrated Succoth by erecting small, temporary, shelters – open to the stars and not built to last – and living in them for the duration of the Festival, as decreed in the Book of Leviticus. It is a reminder on many levels: of the history of a people whose earliest years were nomadic ones, of their utter dependence on God – then, as now – and of the transience of life. And whilst it is an exclusively Jewish festival its meaning extends far beyond that of a single people to encompass us all. For we are all dependent on God: all contingent, all fragile.

Nothing is a more vivid reminder of our dependency than the fact that we require a continuous supply of the two most basic elements in order to survive: water and light. Without these, nothing can grow and nothing can live. Everything that feeds us comes out of the ground, but the ground, too, must be fed. So a Harvest Festival is more than just a reminder. It is a thanksgiving and a prayer too: a prayer that light and water will continue to fall upon the ground, just as it always has. For without this, nothing could be born and nothing could grow. Including us.

During Jesus' time remembrances and rituals involving water and light were a key feature of the Feast of Tabernacles and these centred on the Jerusalem Temple. Each morning during the first seven days of the Feast a procession made its way out of the Temple to the Pool of Siloam. Here, a priest would fill a pitcher with water and the procession would make its way back to the Temple, entering via the Water Gate, and ending at the altar. Once there, amidst much praising and rejoicing, the water would be poured into a small channel at the altar's South side. The choir sang and God was thanked for the harvest, for all was now gathered in. By the time of Jesus, the Feast of Tabernacles had added 'dimensions' as well. In particular, the association had been made with a future time when, like water, God's spirit would be poured out, and thus the line from Isaiah, "With joy you will draw water from the wells of salvation" had also become associated with it (Isaiah 12: 3). Remembrance, transience, thanksgiving, joy and anticipation: these, then, were the things that were uppermost in the minds of the people as they celebrated what Josephus described as 'the holiest and the greatest festival among the Jews' (*Antiquities* 15: 3).

The Last and Greatest Day

But on what John describes as 'the greatest day', no procession to the Pool of Siloam was made. This was the eighth day: the second day of 'solemn rest' as decreed in Leviticus. And it was on this day, John tells us, that Jesus did something very dramatic within the hearing of very many people. It nearly led to his arrest and the result of his words typifies the division that he had already caused.

John tells this story in chapter seven of his gospel and in the chapters leading up to it we have learned that since Jesus' encounter with the woman at Jacob's well his words and actions have aroused deep feelings and some strong opposition: particularly in Judea. In chapter five, for example, we read of a healing of a man by the Pool of Bethesda in Jerusalem. John tells us that this particular healing caused great consternation among some of the people, not least because of the claims that Jesus made on that occasion. In fact, John tells us that some amongst the people sought to kill him then: for healing on the Sabbath and for claiming to be God (John 5: 18). Later we learn that, back in Galilee, Jesus fed five thousand people – one of the few episodes that John's gospel shares with those of Matthew, Mark, and Luke – and that he later walked on water (John 6: 1-16). And throughout, the gospel conveys a strong sense that it is based on the testimony of someone who was *there*. The description of the healing at the Pool of Bethesda, for example, is accompanied by detailed description of both the place and the person involved which suggests that the author has a close acquaintance with both the area in and around Jerusalem and what, for want of a better phrase, we might call the 'local colour' (John 5: 1-5). Even in Galilee the description is, at times, very detailed. John tells us, for example, that on the day after the feeding of the five thousand, 'boats from Tiberias came near the place where they had eaten the bread after the Lord had given thanks' (John 6:23). The 'boats from Tiberias' phrase implies that the author clearly has an eye for detail which in turn suggests either direct acquaintance with the events described or with somebody who witnessed them.

At the beginning of chapter seven of John's gospel we learn that Jesus is being very careful. John tells us that he 'went about in Galilee', knowing that there would be danger if he went to Judea. Urged by his brothers to go to Jerusalem for the Feast of Tabernacles – "that your disciples also may see the works you are doing" - Jesus initially refuses, but later goes: not publicly, but in private' (John 7: 1-10). However, he does not remain incognito for long. By verse 14 of chapter seven we read that in the middle of the feast Jesus is once again in the Temple, teaching. There is yet more controversy and division and the questioning goes on. Where did this uneducated man get all this learning from? Can this be the Messiah? When the Messiah arrives, will he do more signs than this man has done?

Then comes the last and greatest day of the Feast. Jesus chooses this day, the day after the daily water processions have come to an end, to make a remarkable claim. Yet some of his words are hard to understand: not least because it is difficult to work out who they are about. What *is* clear is that on the last and greatest day, perhaps within Temple courts marked by solemnity and silence, Jesus 'cried out' the words: "If anyone thirsts, let him come to me and drink." The next part of this shouted proclamation is problematic and can be rendered in two different ways, depending on punctuation. The first way is the way taken by most translations and typified by the ESV which translates the whole cry as: "If anyone thirsts, let him come to me and drink. Whoever believes in me, as the Scripture has said, 'Out of his heart will flow rivers of living water.'" This rendering has the streams of living water flowing from the *believer* who has first drunk from Jesus. There is, however, a second rendering which gives a somewhat different meaning, and the cry has sometimes been translated as follows: "If anyone thirsts, let him come to me and drink: whoever believes in me. As the scripture has said: 'Out of his heart will flow rivers of living water.'" Here, the *his* is taken to refer to Jesus, not the believer, as in: 'Out of *Jesus'* heart will flow rivers of living water.' Scholars have long debated which rendering is to be preferred, and it makes a difference, as we shall see. In fact, the central theme of this book so far – that John presents Jesus *as* the Temple – will enable us to bring the debate over the meaning of these words to an end once and for all.

Rivers of Living Water

To begin with, it is useful to note that nearly all translations do something very odd. Whether the rivers flow from the believer or Jesus, it is usually the case that it is said to be the *heart* from which they flow. This is how the ESV translates it, and this is the word that is found in most other translations as well. But the actual word that John uses is *koilia*, and this word can be - and is - translated in at least three different ways in the New Testament. Having the basic meaning of 'empty space', it is sometimes used for 'womb', sometimes for 'innermost parts' and sometimes for 'belly'. 'Womb' can be pretty much ruled out as what Jesus meant, particularly if the reference to the source of the living waters is a reference to him, but it would also be rather curious if taken as a reference to the believer. This leaves us with 'innermost parts' or 'belly', and most translations appear to be trying to use 'heart' as a euphemism for 'innermost parts' in an attempt to portray the living waters as coming from *deep within* either the believer or Jesus. But what if 'belly' was used instead? This would make little sense if the living waters are meant to be understood as flowing from the believer. In this instance, Jesus' words would have to be rendered: "If anyone thirsts, let him come to me and drink. Whoever believes in me, as the Scripture has said, 'Out of his belly will flow rivers of living water.'" Why the believers' *belly*? It makes no sense. Besides which, there is no scripture that makes any such reference to water flowing from believers in such a way and from such a source. Would it make more sense, then, if the intended meaning is that rivers of living water flow – or will flow – from *Jesus'* belly?

The Navel of the World

Several things happen if this rendering is preferred. In the ancient world, the temple was often referred to as the 'navel' – or *omphalos* – of creation. The temple at Delphi in Greece, for example, is said to be located where it is because Zeus released two eagles from opposite ends of the earth and commanded them to fly until they met at its centre. They met at Delphi, and Zeus thus placed the 'omphalos stone' there as a sign that this should be where the Temple should be. At Delphi and elsewhere, various traditions' temples were said to stand at the *axis mundi*: the world centre and the meeting place of heaven and earth. Like the navel, such a place was seen as the world's point of origin and beginning: hence the widespread archaeological discovery of 'omphalos stones' at such places. Indeed, the association of temple-location with the world's 'navel' is well-attested and widespread throughout the ancient world and may thus provide some illuminating context on Jesus' claim. It may well be, for example, that Jesus is alluding to what would have been widely-known and understood, and in so doing is appropriating a familiar image in yet another claim to be the Temple. And such, as we have seen, would be very much in keeping with John's consistent assertion that where Jesus was, the Temple was. In fact, this ongoing context lends powerful support to preferring 'navel' to 'innermost parts' as the most accurate translation of the passage, and suggests too that we should read it as referring to Jesus and not the believer. It makes sense of what Jesus says and it fits so well with what has gone before. We have only just, in chapter four, encountered the powerful association of living waters flowing from

Jesus-the-Temple in the story of Jesus' encounter with the Samaritan woman at Jacob's well and thus it should come as no real surprise that we learn something very similar from the events at the Feast of Tabernacles a few chapters on.

Jesus' cry on the last and greatest day of the Feast of Tabernacles is, then, best understood as referring to *him* as the one from whom living waters will flow. That they will flow from his belly – or navel – provides yet another instance of the identification of Jesus with the Temple. That the claim is made in the Temple courts – perhaps close to the altar itself – strengthens the sense that Jesus is being portrayed *as* the Temple, although in what sense we have yet to fully uncover because John has much more to tell. It is clear, though, that the pouring out of water onto the altar within the Temple at the Feast of Tabernacles provides a powerful context for understanding who Jesus is and what he does, and that the opportunity is taken to use the most solemn part of the proceedings to reveal yet again the identification of Jesus with the Temple. Just as physical water has already been used as a way of portraying who Jesus is – in the story of the encounter at Jacob's well – so, now, it is used again to reinforce and make clearer the very same point. Where Jesus is, the Temple is. What Jesus does, the Temple does. But what he is and does takes us very far above and beyond what the physical Temple is and what it can accomplish, and John has yet to fully reveal his hand.

Light of the World

It will be recalled that two realities dominated Succoth: water and light. During this time the Temple precincts were brightly illuminated, and remained so for the majority of the Festival. We read in the Talmud – which, it will be recalled, contains Jewish beliefs and traditions that date back to the time of Jesus – that: 'At the end of the first festival day, [priests and Levites] descended to the Women's Courtyard, where they had made a great improvement. Golden candelabra stood there, on top of each were four bowls, reached by four ladders. Four young priests, carrying 120-log pitchers poured [oil] into each of the bowls. They used worn-out vestures and belts of the priests to light [torches], and every courtyard shone from the lights of the Water-Drawing.' (*Sukka* 5: 512). It must have been a tremendous sight. In a world where light pollution waited several centuries in the future and a moonless night would often be pitch dark, the illumination of the surrounding city from within the Temple precincts must have been both dramatic and highly meaningful. And throughout this celebration of light there was much rejoicing, in keeping with the joyous mood of the Festival. Under the lights there was music and dancing; flute playing and chanting of psalms.

If we assume – as virtually all commentators do – that the episode of the woman caught in adultery did not originally belong between John 7: 53 and 8: 1-11 then there is a close continuity between Jesus' claim to be the source of living waters in verses 37 and 38 in chapter seven and an equally startling claim in chapter eight verse 12. Given what John has been telling us in the run-up to the Festival, it comes as no surprise to learn that Jesus' declaration on the last and greatest day is the occasion of some controversy. John tells us that Jesus' invitation to come to him and drink was 'said about the Spirit, whom those who believed in him were to receive, for as yet the Spirit had not been given because Jesus was not yet glorified.' At this there is yet more division. Is he the Messiah or not? In the midst of this we learn that some want Jesus arrested, 'but no one laid hands on him.' Even officers sent to arrest him are impressed with Jesus' teaching, inviting the scorn of the Pharisees. Jesus finds an ally in Nicodemus who asks "Does our law judge a man without first giving him a hearing and learning what he does?" But this is met with scorn too. "Are you from Galilee too?" the Pharisees ask. "Search and see that no prophet arises from Galilee" (John 7: 40-52).

Omitting the episode of the woman caught in adultery, the very next line following the Pharisees' scorn is another controversial declaration from Jesus. As John tells it: 'Again Jesus spoke to them, saying, "I am the light of the world. Whoever follows me will not walk in darkness, but will have the light of life"' (John 8: 12). We are once again returned to the symbolism of the Feast of Tabernacles. Where lights shine out from the Court of Women into every courtyard in Jerusalem, Jesus claims that *he* is the light of the world, and where he walks there is no darkness: for him or for his followers.

Just as he is the source of living water – the water of life, flowing from the real Temple – now he is portrayed as the source of the world's light. Not a physical light such as that which shone so dazzlingly from the Temple and into every Jerusalem courtyard, but the light of the world, shining from the *real* Temple to give light to everyone who would otherwise walk in darkness. Seizing the opportunity provided by the Feast of Tabernacles, Jesus appears in John as the source of what that Feast celebrated. And of course, what that Feast celebrated was centred on what happened in the Temple, what was done there, and what came from there. It is as if John is shifting the focus yet again away from the actual, physical, Temple, and onto Jesus. Somehow, he seems to be saying, the Temple is being displaced. Jesus is the Temple now. What it did, he did. What it does, he does. What it will do, he has started to do and will continue to do.

At this point, the images have already been stacking up. Jesus is the tabernacling presence of God. He is the one on whom angels will ascend and descend. His body will be the rebuilt Temple, somehow put together again three days after its destruction. He is the source of living water. He is the navel of creation. And now he is the light of the world. Jesus *as* the Temple: it is a building, rising, theme. John is opening a door wider and wider, using every powerful historical, cultural and religious image and tool at his disposal and at each crucial point in his gospel we are shown something more. It is a brilliant strategy; and he returns to it with devastating effect in chapter ten of his gospel.

By the time we reach that chapter a shadow has deepened over proceedings. John has consistently pointed forwards from almost the very beginning of his gospel to its end, and references to Jesus' 'hour', his 'lifting up' and his 'glorification' have all been devices that he has used to point the reader to Jesus' fate. That he will ultimately fall victim to his enemies has been further indicated by the ever-increasing opposition that he has faced. His claim at the Feast of Tabernacles arouses the by-now predictable controversy. Insults are traded. "You are of your father the devil, and your will is to do your father's desires" says Jesus in chapter 8 verse 44. "Are we not right in saying that you are a Samaritan and have a demon?" comes the rhetorical reply. A healing of a man born blind in chapter nine elicits further controversy. By the opening verses of chapter ten Jesus is describing himself as

"The good shepherd" who "lays down his life for his sheep" and the 'laying down of his life' theme continues throughout chapter ten's opening verses. In verse 17 we learn that Jesus lays down his life "that I may take it up again." In the following verse he adds "No one takes it from me, but I lay it down of my own accord. I have authority to lay it down, and I have authority to take it up again." This enigmatic series of declarations elicits more division. Yet the reader, once again knowing more than the characters, scents where things are going. A life will be lost. Yet the one who loses it seems firmly in control. Indeed, he claims the authority to take it up again: an authority derived, in turn, from his Father.

The Feast of Dedication

By the time we arrive at John chapter ten verse 22 we are at the Feast of Dedication. It is winter, and Jesus is teaching in Solomon's portico, a covered area to the extreme East of the Temple Mount overlooking the Kidron valley. The seasons are proceeding with the usual regularity, and with them the Feasts and Festivals of the Jewish calendar. And Temple life goes on. In fact, apart from a relatively brief period in the second century BCE, there had been daily sacrifices in it for nearly 600 years by this point. For nearly six centuries pilgrims had flocked there to celebrate Passover and the other festivals and the High Priest had gone into the Holy of Holies on the Day of Atonement to sprinkle the sacrificial blood to plead atonement for the sins of the people. Nearly 600 years of hymns, worship, sacrifice, festivals, and slaughter in the Jerusalem Temple. Generation after generation had gazed at it, lived with it and marvelled at it. It must have seemed like the one permanent, unshakable and immovable thing in their otherwise precarious and difficult lives.

But for three years it all stopped. Between 167 and 164 BCE dreadful things happened in the Temple. Antiochus Epiphanes was a king in Syria and he loved all things Greek. He also hated all things Jewish. Including the Temple. In 170 BCE he attacked Jerusalem. 80,000 Jews perished or were sold into slavery. The Jewish law – the Torah – was banned. It became against the law even to be circumcised, and those who had their babies circumcised were crucified with their babies around their necks. Yet Antiochus reserved his greatest ire and loudest mockery for the Jews' holiest precincts. He plundered the Temple treasury and stole a huge amount of money. The Temple chambers, where once things like scripture scrolls were kept, were turned into brothels. He turned the sacred altar, where sacrifice had been made twice daily for nigh-on six centuries, into an altar to the god Zeus. And he continued to have sacrifices made. But instead of bulls and lambs he sacrificed pigs.

For three years absolute, utter, and deliberate blasphemy reigned. Until 164 BC when a brave group of Jews led by Judas Maccabeus and his brother fought back. They defeated the blasphemer and took back the Temple and consecrated it once more to reverse the desecration that had been forced on it by a man who himself had claimed to be divine. They got rid of the brothels and brought back the Torah scrolls. They replaced all the priests' robes. They replaced all the utensils, including those that were used to make sacrifices with. And they completely rebuilt the altar. Finally, on 25th Kislev 164 BC, it was formally consecrated. It was God's House again and they thereafter decided that every year, for eight days, there would be a special festival known as the Feast of Dedication. 1 Maccabees 4:59 sums up the decree: '[T]he days of the dedication of the altar should be kept in their season from year to year, by the space of eight days, from the five and twentieth day of the month of Kislev, with gladness and joy.'

He Whom the Father Consecrated

This, then, is the context for the next part of the Gospel of John. It is the Feast of Dedication and three things are uppermost on everybody's mind: blasphemy, consecration, and the return of the light to Israel. Jesus takes advantage during the winter months of the shelter offered by the colonnades of Solomon's Portico to continue to teach his disciples. Controversy predictably ensues. 'The Jews' demand to know if he is the Messiah. Given that he has already loudly and publicly claimed to be the one who will rebuild the Temple it is a somewhat odd – even redundant – question, to which they have already received an answer. Indeed, Jesus' reply to the demand suggests a certain exasperation: "I told you, and you do not believe." He then reminds them of his "good works", daring to suggest that they do not believe because they are not his sheep. Again, Ezekiel hangs heavily over the story, but whereas in that book it is God who declares "Behold, I judge between sheep and sheep" (Ezekiel 34: 17) now it is Jesus who makes a very similar claim: "The works that I do in my Father's name bear witness about me, but you do not believe because you are not among my sheep. My sheep hear my voice, and I know them, and they follow me. I give them eternal life, and they will never perish, and no one will snatch them out of my hand. My Father, who has given them to me, is greater than all, and no-one is able to snatch them out of the Father's hand." (John 10: 25-9). It is a remarkable claim, and the reference to choosing some sheep and rejecting others is a claim that could not have fallen on deaf ears. Its climax, however, is shocking in its directness: "I and the Father are one." This is too much for Jesus' opponents who, obviously aware of the import and significance of such a claim at such a time, pick up stones to stone him for blasphemy. Jesus asks them which of his good works he is to be stoned for. "It is not for a good work that we are going to stone you but for blasphemy, because you, being a man, make yourself God" they reply. There follows a typically rabbinic response from Jesus and it is complex. John writes: 'Jesus answered them, "Is it not written in your Law, 'I said, you are gods'? If he called them gods to whom the word of God came – and scripture cannot be broken – [why] do you say of him whom the Father consecrated and sent into the world, 'You are blaspheming', because I said 'I am the Son of God'?" Given that the word 'gods' – *elohim* – here is from Psalm 82: 6 where it is used to denote human judges, Jesus seems to be saying, in effect, 'If those judges to whom the word of God came could be called 'gods', why can't I call myself the Son of God?' As interesting as this is, it is the authority he claims to be able to say it which is of greater interest. He is able to say this, he asserts, because he is the one "whom the Father consecrated and sent into the world."

At a Feast in which consecration of the Temple resonates in thought and memory, Jesus' words are clearly designed to recall to mind what was done to the Temple in the aftermath of its three-year desecration. John even uses the same word for consecrate – *hagiazo* – that is used in the description of the consecration of the Temple in 1 Maccabees 4: 48: 'They also rebuilt the sanctuary and the interior of the Temple, and consecrated the courts.' But what does Jesus mean? Again, it is possible to view his enigmatic response to his accusers on more than one level. To claim to be consecrated by the Father may mean no more than to claim a special anointing or blessing or mission. But within the context of John's unfolding gospel, a deeper reading inevitably presents itself. Just as the physical Temple was consecrated in the time of the Maccabees, so is the 'new' Temple consecrated also. But this is a very special Temple and it thus receives a special consecration. It comes directly from the Father, and gives legitimation and authority to what that Temple says and does. The import of Jesus' claim to have been consecrated in this way is not lost on his opponents. John tells us that 'Again they sought to arrest him, but he escaped from their hands.'

Across the Jordan

Almost at the very end of the story we read something very interesting. In verse 40, following Jesus' 'escape', we read how 'He went away again across the Jordan to the place where John had been baptizing at first, and there he remained.' (John 10:40). Just a few chapters earlier in John, we read that he was in the Temple at the Feast of Tabernacles, teaching. We recall in John 7: 37 that Jesus stood up on the last and greatest day of that feast and shouted "If anyone thirsts, let him come to me and drink". By the beginning of chapter ten he has moved out of the Temple and he is in the colonnade of Solomon, as far east across the Temple precinct as he could possibly be. And by the end of the story he has moved even further east, across the Jordan, having left not just the Temple precinct but Jerusalem itself. Given that leaving the Temple to the east was how God departed it in Ezekiel chapter ten verses 18-19, it is possible that John is making a similar claim, showing at this point that the divine presence of Jesus left the Temple of Herod in a similar, parallel, way. This might be pushing things too far, but the fact remains that the Gospel of John undergoes a profound 'shift' at this point. By the end of the tenth chapter of John's gospel we are approaching endgame, and the shadow of death looms ever larger over the narrative. Given what we have seen up to this point, it is not surprising that

John's presentation of Jesus as the Temple is about to undergo a profound shift also.

Interlude

Buying the World a Coke

One of the 100 largest companies in the world with annual sales totalling tens of billions of dollars, the Coca-Cola company has long been at the leading edge of worldwide marketing and sales, and many of its advertising campaigns have successfully tapped into the 'global psyche' as few others have done. Who could forget, for example, what has become known as the 'Hilltop Commercial'? Possibly the world's first truly multi-cultural advertisement, this short film released in 1971 featured young people of all colours and nationalities standing shoulder to shoulder on a sunny hilltop and singing "in perfect harmony" of how they'd like to buy the world a Coke. It was, they sang, the "real thing"; a refrain that recurred throughout the song and which featured in the company's advertising slogan for that year. It looks dated now, but at the time it was a game-changer.

Slogans sell products, and nobody has understood this better than the Coca-Cola company: hence their massive annual sales. In the U.S alone, Coca-Cola has had 57 sales slogans since 1886 and in the U.K and Canada it has had a similar number. These have varied and have in many instances reflected how times have changed. The first slogan, in 1886, simply said 'Drink Coca-Cola and Enjoy It.' In 1904 would-be purchasers were urged to drink it because it was 'Delicious and Refreshing.' By 1906 it was 'The Great National Temperance Beverage.' By the time of 1907's simple 'Three Million a Day' slogan, sales were clearly dictating the way the product was being presented, and 1925's 'Six Million a Day' slogan showed how these had soared in the intervening years.

It's the Real Thing!

By 1941, however, things had taken something of a turn. That year's slogan – 'Coca-Cola is Coke!' – revealed that perhaps the company was feeling the impact of its competitors on the sales of its premier brand. 1942's slogan - 'The Only Thing Like Coca-Cola is Coke!' - provided further evidence that Coke wasn't having the whole market to itself during the war years. In fact, the manufacturer's claim that Coca Cola was in some sense the 'Real Thing' fairly dominated slogans in the post-war years. So, for example, in 1967, 'It's the Real Thing!' was duly the slogan *du jour*, and one which was still much to the fore four years later in 1971's Hilltop Commercial. By 1981 this had become, simply, 'Coke is It!' and by 1998 Coca-Cola was 'Always the Real Thing!' By 2003, the slogan simply said 'Real.' And by 2005 consumers were urged to 'Make it Real.'

The Coca-Cola company's post-war preference for marketing its product in various ways as the 'Real Thing' is an interesting one. On the surface, it can simply be seen as a snappy way of saying 'accept no substitutes' in a market increasingly populated by new and rival products, all trying to steal Coke's 'crown' and using the 'Cola' name in various different guises. But does this fact *alone* explain the number of times and the various different ways in which Coke has been said to be 'real'? On a deeper level, human beings have always looked for the 'real thing'. So, for example, we look for 'real love' and when we find it, we say of the object of our affections that he or she is the 'real thing.' We talk about the 'real McCoy.' We urge our errant friends to 'get real.' Dreamers are often told to live in the 'real world.' And so on.

Philosophy, Science, and the 'Real Thing'

Indeed, finding the 'real thing' has been something of a fixation for philosophers, theologians and scientists since the birth of each of their disciplines. Scientists, for example, have long been fascinated with the 'stuff' out of which the universe is made and the basic laws that govern it. Quantum physics, they say, shows 'reality' to be 'weirder' than we can ever imagine. Philosophers have shared this ongoing concern with the 'real'. One of the founding fathers of Western philosophy, Plato, thought that the world that our senses shows us is deeply *un*real, and that reality exists on another plane or level altogether and accessible only with the mind and by a select few. For him, reality is essentially hidden, and we are wrong when we mistake 'mere appearances' for the 'real thing'. Perhaps, then, *this* is what so many Coca-Cola slogans have sought to tap into: our yearning to see past appearances and 'tune in' to what is really, absolutely, and ultimately *real*. 'Coke can give you this', the company proclaims, despite the sheer improbability of this really being so.

John and the 'Real Thing'

In his concern to show how Jesus is the Temple, there is a very real sense in which John repeatedly tries to show that Jesus is the 'Real Thing'. And this, as we have been seeing, is a most remarkable claim and one which John claims completely confused many of Jesus' contemporaries: including, during his physical, earthly, lifetime, the disciples themselves. As previous chapters have shown, the Temple at the time of Jesus was a vast building; a magnificent edifice atop the highest point of Israel's holiest city. It needed thousands of people just to operate. It had its own police force. It was central to Israel's worship, her calendar, and her entire cultural, national, and spiritual life. By the time of Jesus' demonstration at Passover it had taken 46 years to build and was still unfinished. Without it there could be no annual commemoration of the events of Israel's history, no proper system or practice of sacrifice, and no official Torah-sanctioned 'mechanism' by which sins could be forgiven. Historically it had been the place of God's presence in the midst of His people, the locus of His revelation, and the repository of Israel's most sacred treasures. At the time of Jesus it must have seemed unmoveable and indestructible: a fixed point around which the annual life of an entire people revolved. There was nothing like it anywhere else on earth and it marked - as it always had - nothing less than the point, for Jews, from which God created the world. It was the *omphalos*; the navel. It was the centre of the entire created order. The entire cosmos revolved around it. And Jesus, says John, claimed to *be* it.

Little wonder that the response of 'the Jews' to Jesus' claim to be the Temple was one of mockery, sarcasm, and incredulity. Yet what has been emerging in this book, and what will emerge with even greater vividness and detail in the chapters that follow, is that in claiming to be the Temple, Jesus did not simply claim 'equivalence' to it or some sort of equal status with it. As startling as it at first seems, there is a crucial sense in which Jesus claimed to stand in relation to the Temple as the reality stands in relation to a mere appearance; as if the Temple, magnificent and massive in its size and importance, was but an unreal 'shadow' or 'copy' of him. This is a stupendous claim; going beyond, even, the claim that he will rebuild, supplant, or outlast it. That all of these are implied in his claim to be the 'real thing' is not in doubt. Yet Jesus, according to John, goes even further than this. They are both Temples, he says, but of the two, Jesus is the *more real*.

This recognition will be one which the next chapters will reinforce time and time again, but in deeper and ever more surprising ways. In the next chapter it is made explicit in one of Jesus' most famous 'I am' sayings. In the chapters that follow we will see it in relation to two of the holiest of the Jewish festivals, both centred on the Temple: Passover and the Day of Atonement. By the time we reach the end of the gospel we will also have been confronted with a remarkable and wholly unexpected 'twist' as we continue to uncover the shocking implications of what John goes to such great lengths to show us: that to have seen Jesus was to have seen the Temple in its fullest, most real, sense, and that the Temple that stood atop Mount Moriah during his lifetime was to Jesus as a copy is to an original.

Chapter Six: "I Am the True Vine"

"I am the true vine, and my Father is the vine dresser"

John 15: 1

Darkening Clouds

In John's gospel, time and place are everything. As we have already seen, when and where something happens is crucial for him, and his placing of events in time and space enables him to 'open up' additional layers of meaning underneath the surface of his narrative. This is particularly the case as the gospel moves towards its climax. With death hanging ever heavier over events, the timing and placement of them becomes ever more important.

Approximately half way through his gospel John tells us that with the raising of Lazarus from the dead the polarisation of opinion regarding Jesus reaches a new extreme. As support for him builds, so opposition hardens, and the shadow of death falls more darkly still. There has been trouble behind and even more trouble lies ahead and that Jesus is in danger is apparent both from his own actions and from what his friends and enemies say and do. So, for example, when in chapter eleven he decides to go to Bethany in Judea to raise Lazarus from the dead it is Thomas who remarks to his fellow disciples: "Let us also go, that we may die with him" (John 11: 16). The raising that follows only serves to raise opposition to fever pitch and by the time we have reached virtually the end of the chapter John tells us that Jesus no longer walked openly among 'the Jews' but went into the wilderness to a town called Ephraim (John 11: 54). We also learn that Passover is at hand, and with this comes the realisation that Jesus is a hot topic of conversation among those who, standing in the Temple, ponder among themselves whether or not he will attend. At the very end of chapter eleven we learn that the topic is hot indeed, given the fact that 'the chief priests and the Pharisees had given orders that if anyone knew where [Jesus] was, he should let them know, so that they might arrest him' (John 11: 57).

By the beginning of chapter twelve we learn that it is six days before Passover and 'Jesus therefore came to Bethany' (John 12: 1). Given the closeness of Bethany to Jerusalem it is now clear to the reader that the question of whether or not Jesus will attend the Holy City for the Passover celebrations has been answered. At Bethany, Mary, the sister of Martha and Lazarus, anoints Jesus with a pound of expensive ointment made, John says, from pure nard. It is a beautiful scene, marred only by Judas's objection to what he sees as waste. Surely this nard would have been better sold and the money given to the poor! But John 'buts in' to the narrative to explain the objection: it turns out that Judas's indignation was caused by nothing more than his own greed and selfishness. He was, John tells us, in charge of the money bag and 'used to help himself to what was put into it.' And then the meaning of events is made clearer still. "Leave her alone", says Jesus "so that she may keep it for the day of my burial. For the poor you always have with you, but you do not always have me" (John 12: 1-8).

Soon after this we learn that not even Lazarus is safe from those whose ire has been provoked by Jesus' ministry. John tells us that the chief priests made plans to put him to death as well, on account of the fact that his miraculous raising from death had simply added to the number of those who believed in Jesus (John 12: 9-11). But the focus swiftly shifts back to John's main subject. His description of Jesus' triumphal entry into Jerusalem for his final Passover mirrors in key respects the descriptions given in Matthew, Mark and Luke. There are cries of acclaim accompanied by waving of palm branches as Jesus rides into Jerusalem on a donkey. John again reminds us of the fact that the raising of Lazarus has been instrumental in raising this support for Jesus to fever pitch (John 12: 12-19). And there are yet more references to Jesus' impending fate. In chapter 12: 31-33 John makes this as clear as he can in his own commentary on Jesus' words. Following a voice from Heaven (which only some can identify as a voice), Jesus says: "This voice has come for your sake, not mine. Now is the judgement of this world; now will the ruler of this world be cast out. And I, when I am lifted up from the earth, will draw all people to myself." To which John adds, simply: 'He said this to show by what kind of death he was going to die.'

The beginning of chapter thirteen begins a new 'phase' in John's gospel: one marked by privacy and increased intimacy between Jesus and the disciples together with ever-clearer disclosure from him to them concerning what is to come. It leads into a long passage and it is difficult to see where it ends. It is possible to read it in such a way that it only ends when the 'countdown' to Jesus' crucifixion begins with his arrest at the beginning of chapter eighteen although a 'break' in the narrative at the end of chapter fourteen makes it very likely that two distinct occasions separated by a short interlude provide two distinct contexts for what Jesus has to say, as we shall see.

Foot washing and the Father's House

Given that this book has Jesus as the Temple as its focus it may seem odd to pass over in relative silence two incidents that have traditionally been seen to equate them both – at least, to an extent – but there are good reasons for doing exactly this. The first of these is the well-known episode in John chapter thirteen in which Jesus washes the disciples' feet as an example of how they should be towards one another. This has sometimes been seen as a ritual in which Jesus consecrates a new priesthood, given that in Exodus God tells Moses that Aaron and his sons must wash their hands and feet before going into the tent of meeting or offering sacrifice outside the Tabernacle at the altar. Given that the practice of priestly washing in order to consecrate them for their duties persisted throughout the Temple's subsequent history it has sometimes been suggested that in this episode John is portraying Jesus as consecrating a new priesthood for a new Temple by washing their feet. Yet it is hard to make this parallel work. For one thing, there is no description of Jesus washing his disciples' *hands* in this passage, yet this is clearly part of the preparation for priestly service given by God to Moses in Exodus (Exodus 30: 19). For another, it is likely that the actual meaning of Jesus' action in John is simply that which John himself gives: that Jesus meant it as an example of service which his disciples were to emulate. There is none of the layered symbolism that we have seen previously in John and which indicates a deeper meaning, apart from that implied in Jesus' assertion that not every one of his disciples was clean, and that the disciples only realised who it was – Judas – later.

Another incident which can also be passed over in relative silence occurs in John chapter fourteen where Jesus promises his disciples that there are many rooms in his Father's House and that he is going to prepare a place for them. That the Temple was frequently described as God's House and that Jesus describes the Temple as his 'Father's House' elsewhere in John makes a strong case on the surface for seeing this as a reference to the earthly – or perhaps a heavenly – Temple. The occasion seems identical to that of the earlier foot washing and the meaning seems to be that Jesus is going to the 'heavenly Temple' to make rooms for his disciples to join him in it. However, once again it is not apparent that this is a reference to Jesus being in any sense equated with the Temple and the use of *oikia* – meaning house*hold* - for 'house' here has suggested to some recent commentators that the passage is in fact drawing on notions of middle-eastern hospitality in its portrayal of Jesus as one who is inviting the disciples into the new intimacy of his Father's household. That foot washing was typically done on welcoming somebody into a new household ties this episode to the foot washing that preceded it and reinforces the message that a new intimacy with Jesus and the Father is being introduced as the gospel reaches its climax.

"Rise, let us go from here"

It seems, then, that neither John's account of the foot washing episode nor his description of Jesus' promise to the disciples to prepare places in his Father's House for them contribute directly to his 'temple-centric' theme. However, the episode which follows on from these gives much stronger grounds for supposing that John is making another reference to Jesus as the Temple. Having promised that his departure to the Father will be the occasion for the sending of the Spirit, Jesus stresses the importance of love, pronounces peace over his disciples, and warns that "the ruler of this world is coming" (John 14: 30). He then apparently brings a long sequence of teachings to a close. "Rise" he says, "let us go from here" (John 14: 31). It is an odd, blunt, and strangely anti-climactic ending to a remarkable series of discourses and yet it seems clear that it is intended to mark the end of one extended episode and to show that what follows occurs in a different place and at a different, albeit slightly later, time.

The episode that follows is, in fact, an extended *saying* which appears abruptly and apparently without introduction. It is well-known and has been much-discussed, although exactly *where* Jesus says it will need to be carefully 'unpacked'. Seemingly straight after the "Rise, let us go from here", John tells us that Jesus says:

"I am the true vine, and my Father is the vine dresser. Every branch in me that does not bear fruit he takes away, and every branch that does bear fruit he prunes, that it may bear more fruit. Already you are clean because of the word that I have spoken to you. Abide in me, and I in you. As the branch cannot bear fruit by itself, unless it abides in the vine, neither can you, unless you abide in me. I am the vine, you are the branches. Whoever abides in me and I in him, he it is that bears much fruit, for apart from me you can do nothing. If anyone does not abide in me he is thrown away like a branch and withers; and the branches are gathered, thrown into the fire, and burned. If you abide in me, and my words abide in you, ask whatever you wish, and it will be done for you. By this my father is glorified, that you bear much fruit and so prove to be my disciples. As the Father has loved me, so have I loved you. Abide in my love. If you keep my commandments, you will abide in my love, just as I have kept my Father's commandments and abide in his love. These things I have spoken to you, that my joy may be in you, and that your joy may be full" (John 15: 1-11).

Whilst no reference is made by John to where this teaching was given it is clear that it has a number of references within the gospel overall and elsewhere and that these might provide clues to its overall meaning and even to the location at which it was given. Firstly, and most obviously, it looks like a continuation of what has immediately preceded it. As we have already seen, in the previous two chapters Jesus has been promising a special closeness with his disciples. He has promised a place in his Father's House(hold). He has talked enigmatically about a coming day when "you will know that I am in my Father, and you in me, and I in you" (John 14: 20). He has talked equally enigmatically about both he and his Father making their home with anyone who loves him. And now he talks about this special closeness in a different way and using a vivid image. The disciples, he says, are to see themselves as his branches and himself as the vine and his Father as the vinedresser. It is a very arresting symbol of closeness and mutual interaction and one which would have been very familiar to anyone who lived close to the land and knew its ways. Without the vinedresser the vine has no chance of bearing fruit and the branches cannot bear fruit independently of the vine. The whole is one organic unit and will only be fruitful as such. Take away the vinedresser or the branch from the vine and nothing will be produced. Even the fruitless branch is good for nothing beyond being used as kindling. In fact, there is a real sense in which the image is one of life versus death and that the passage relates to this as well as to the importance of abiding. You will only live, says Jesus, if you are 'joined' to me and my Father. Without us you are like a dead branch: nothing but fuel for the fire. Seen in this sense, it is tempting to see the right context for consideration of this passage as lying in the teachings concerning eternal life that run throughout John's gospel, as well as the teachings about Father-Son-Disciple intimacy that have been to the fore in the previous chapters.

The Vineyard of the Lord

But other contexts present themselves also, equally deserving of consideration. For centuries before Jesus' time the vine had been a very frequently used symbol to denote the people of Israel and their 'fruitfulness' as the people of God and it is an Old Testament image that recurs over and over again. Psalm 80 makes particularly vivid use of it. In verse 8 of that psalm, for example, God is addressed as one who "bought a vine out of Egypt" and as One who "drove out the nations and planted it." God's care for this vine is stressed, as is its one-time flourishing: "You cleared the ground for it; it took deep root and filled the land. The mountains were covered with its shade, the mighty cedars with its branches. It sent out its branches to the sea and its shoots to the River" (Psalm 80: 9-11). The next verses make clear, however, that this psalm is not one of celebration but lament. Will the Lord of hosts not save Israel? Why do its walls lie in ruins "so that all who pass along the way pick her fruit?" The psalmist implores: "Turn again, O God of hosts! Look down from heaven, and see; have regard for this vine, the stock that your right hand planted, and for the son whom you made strong for yourself. They have burned it with fire; they have cut it down; may they perish at the rebuke of your face!" (Psalm 80: 14-16). Implied throughout this psalm is the sad fact that this vine lies amongst ruined walls because of God's anger with Israel. Thus, the psalmist writes: "O Lord God of hosts, how long will you be angry with your people's prayers?" (Psalm 80: 4).

This is a consistent theme throughout the Old Testament. Vine imagery is used to describe Israel as one who has gone astray and grown wild and is thus needful of rebuke. God's word to Jeremiah typifies this: "I planted you as a choice vine, wholly of pure seed. How then have you turned degenerate and become a wild vine?" (Jeremiah 2: 21). It is once again Ezekiel, though, whose text overhangs John's most closely and densely, and the dramatic use of vine imagery in Ezekiel 15: 1-6 is starkly reminiscent of that found at the beginning of John 15:

> "And the word of the Lord came to me: "Son of man, how does the wood of the vine surpass any wood, the vine branch that is among the trees of the forest? Is wood taken from it to make anything? Do people take a peg from it to hang any vessel on it? Behold, it is given to the fire for fuel. When the fire has consumed both ends of it, and the middle of it is charred, is it useful for anything? Behold, when it was whole, it was used for nothing. How much less, when the fire has consumed it and it is charred, can it ever be used for anything! Therefore thus says the Lord God: Like the wood of the vine among the trees of the forest, which I have given to the fire for fuel, so have I given up the inhabitants of Jerusalem" (Ezekiel 15: 1-6).

Clearly, this extract from Ezekiel stands in the background of Jesus' claim to be a vine apart from which the branches are fit for burning only. The closely shared imagery of the vine and the burning fate of a useless branch makes this virtually certain. Not for the first time, the writer of John's gospel has Ezekiel firmly in mind. Is this, then, a clue to the full meaning of Jesus' claim to be the *true* vine? Read like this, Israel becomes a false or degenerate vine, and Jesus and his disciples are shown to be its replacement: a sort of 'New Israel' which the Father will lovingly tend so that it brings forth ever more fruit, and for which dependence on Jesus is an absolute, life-giving, necessity.

The Golden Vine

This has been a popular interpretation of the passage that we are considering. But is this all there is to it? Once again - and as ever with John - it is at least possible that another, deeper, meaning lies under the surface. Might our ongoing exploration of Jesus as the Temple provide it? Firstly, it is interesting to recall that by the time of Jesus – and during his lifetime – the Temple atop Mount Moriah was a massive and splendid complex of buildings with the Holy Place and the Holy of Holies at its most sacred heart, as we have seen. Little wonder, then, that such an incredible place would have the ultimate in decoration and adornment and various writings from the period describe one piece of decoration in particular. Jewish historian Josephus – who, it will be recalled, was ideally placed to provide reliable and detailed eyewitness testimony to the Temple's dimensions, magnificence, and function at the time of Jesus - writes in his *Antiquities* that 'Above the gate of the Temple were golden vines and grape clusters as large as a man.' (*Antiquities*, 15, xi, 3). The gate he is referring to is the entrance to the Holy Place and Holy of Holies, to which access was restricted to the Priests and High Priest respectively: the 'Temple Proper', in other words, which was modelled after the detailed instructions given to Moses on Mount Sinai. This golden vine was clearly a magnificent sight. The most striking decoration on the Temple façade, it hung right above the doors to its *naos*, or sanctuary. The doors to this sanctuary were themselves covered in gold and the vine may have hung from free-standing columns on either side of the doorway: this is not entirely clear, despite scattered references to it in Josephus, the Midrashic tractate *Middot*, and the Roman historian Tacitus.

What *is* clear is that the vine was a striking and massive aspect of the Temple during the lifetime of Jesus, and that he and his disciples would have gazed upon it on many occasions. The grape clusters were themselves the size of a person, as Josephus avows, and the whole was an ornate and expanding golden frieze which was continually added to, as funds allowed. Wealthy persons were able to bring gifts which were added to the vine, and in this way its golden tendrils, leaves and grapes provided an ever-expanding tableau.

Is Jesus' claim in John's gospel to be the true vine a reference to this? The objection might be raised that 'true vine' is simply a metaphor being used to denote Jesus and his disciples as a 'true' or 'replacement' Israel. After all, the vine as a symbol for Israel was ubiquitous during Jesus' day, as we have already noted. In addition to the scriptures it appeared on coins, burial places and in art. But it is significant that, as with the other 'I am' sayings, the use of the definite article – 'I am *the* true vine' – is used. Several things are important to note in the light of this and they have significant bearing on the passage that we are considering. Firstly, the 'I am' phrase in Greek - *ego eimi* – is a frequent *motif* which runs throughout John's gospel. Previously it has been used to denote Jesus' claim to be the bread of life, the light of the world, the gate, the good shepherd, the resurrection and the life, and the way, the truth, and the life, and now, in its seventh and final appearance, it is being used to denote his claim to be the true vine. And throughout, where the phrase *ego eimi* is used with a predicate following – as in 'I am the good shepherd' - there is always the definite article: 'the'. This is interesting, given that predicate nouns in Greek usually *lack* the definite article. Where the definite article is used it carries the claim beyond 'mere' metaphor and, instead, is showing that the subject is identical with that to which he or she is referring. In the case of Jesus, therefore, a claim such as 'I am the light of the world' is a claim to be not just *like* light but to be the *actual* light: however strange this sounds. In the same way, the claim 'I am the gate' is a claim to be not *like* a gate for his sheep but is a claim to be the *actual* gate: whatever this may mean. In the current context, therefore, where Jesus is claiming to be the true vine he seems to be at least claiming to be, not just *like* a vine – conceivably the very vine that hung above the Temple's *naos* – but to actually *be* it. Thus, there is a crucial sense here that in claiming to be *the* vine he is once again equating himself with the Temple: specifically, with something that hung over and was fixed upon the entrance to that Temple's holiest spaces, and thus a part of it. When this observation is located within the ongoing 'flow' of episodes in John where Jesus as the Temple is a frequently-encountered *motif* it becomes a striking addition to an ongoing and consistent theme – however strange it may sound when understood in this way.

The True Vine

Yet there is more to it even than this. Included in Jesus' claim to be *the* vine is the claim that he is, in fact, the *true* vine. The word for 'true' here is *alethinos* and it is found throughout John's gospel where it typically conveys one of a group of closely-related meanings such as 'true', 'genuine', or 'real'. So, for example, in John 1: 9 Jesus is described as the 'true [or genuine or real] light which gives life to everyone.' In John 4: 23 Jesus tells the Samaritan woman that "[T]he hour is coming, and is now here, when the true [or genuine or real] worshippers will worship the Father in spirit and truth." In John 6: 32 Jesus tells his listeners that "my Father gives you the true [or genuine or real] bread from heaven." And in John 15: 1, in the passage we have been considering, Jesus says "I am the true [or genuine or real] vine, and my Father is the vinedresser." The inclusion of *alethinos* here takes the meaning even further away from a metaphorical or allegorical one. Instead, it is as if Jesus is saying that in the most literal sense he is the true or real or genuine vine, in contrast to all others. This could certainly be taken to mean that he is the true or real or genuine *Israel*, but given what we know about the Temple's most striking and richly symbolic adornment above the gates to its holiest places another meaning becomes very possible. It is as if Jesus is saying: 'You see that? *I am* the real one.' This would certainly be in keeping with what John has been at pains to tell us up to this point.

A Journey at Night

In order to grasp the actual, intended, meaning of the passage, it would be useful to know where, exactly, it took place. We know *when* it took place, because it is located in John's gospel after the events in the upper room on the night before Passover and immediately before a further series of teachings which climax with what has traditionally – although for no obvious reason – been termed 'The High Priestly Prayer'. There then immediately follows a vivid and detailed description of Jesus' betrayal and arrest in John chapter eighteen which will be examined in the next chapter of this book.

One clue as to *where* the events of chapters fifteen through to seventeen of John may have taken place might be found at the end of chapter fourteen. As we have seen, that chapter ends abruptly with Jesus saying "Rise, let us go from here." It is likely, therefore, that we are intended to conclude that what occurs immediately afterwards – Jesus' teaching including his claim to be the true vine – happens somewhere else. We know that it is Passover time, and that during Jesus' day the city gates were kept open all night to allow passage into and out of the city for the many thousands of pilgrims that travelled to Jerusalem for the festival. Might it have been the case that Jesus and his disciples *stopped* somewhere *en route* from the location of the events recounted in chapters thirteen and fourteen to the events in the garden surrounding his betrayal and that the subsequent teachings occurred *where* they stopped? Or that some of them did? And might that place have been the Temple or its immediate vicinity? Whilst obviously we cannot know this with certainty it would at the very least have provided a likely 'trigger' or context for a teaching which included the claim to be the true vine. But even if such was *not* the case, this chapter has done much to show that the magnificent golden vine above the Temple's holiest places provides a likely backdrop that allows us to unlock the full meaning of the claim, even if it did not provide the actual physical location for the actual teaching.

Unlocking the Implications

"I am the *true* vine; the *real* vine; the *genuine* vine." Jesus' words can be translated in any of these three ways, but whichever way they are translated the result is a claim characterised by its *strangeness*. Little wonder, then, that it is commonly read as some kind of allegory and interpreted as if it is referring to Jesus and the disciples as a 'new' or 'supplanting' Israel. But why *should* we read it in this way? Whilst, as we have seen, Israel-as-vine is commonly encountered in the Old Testament and elsewhere, the notion of Jesus and his disciples as a 'future Israel' seems not to be something that John or any other New Testament writer makes anything of anywhere else. Taken as another literal claim to be the Temple, however, it stands in real continuity with what John has repeatedly gone to great and ingenious lengths to stress earlier in the gospel and with what he will return to in what lies ahead.

We have yet to fully consider the implications of the claim, however, and this is in large part because John withholds their full nature, scope and reverberations for the final, crowning, events of his gospel. In what sense might we see Jesus as a true, real or genuine vine – and, by extension, a true, real or genuine *Temple*? The corollary of the claim is that the actual Temple is false, unreal or even fake. That it is lacking or not good enough or that it stands in relation to Jesus as a copy stands to an original. Whichever way we turn this teaching to the light, its strangeness is almost dazzling. Yet it is of a piece with what John has told us before. And as his gospel reaches its climax and the final, dramatic, events unfold, the full implications of Jesus' remarkable claim will become clear. John has much left to reveal, and he keeps his most startling insights until the timing is such that they are able to emerge with a clarity that is as vivid as it is unexpected.

Chapter Seven: 'He Who Saw It Has Borne Witness'

Since it was the day of Preparation, and so that the bodies would not remain on the cross on the Sabbath (for that Sabbath was a high day), the Jews asked Pilate that their legs might be broken and they might be taken away. So the soldiers came and broke the legs of the first, and of the other who had been crucified with him. But when they came to Jesus and saw that he was already dead, they did not break his legs. But one of the soldiers pierced his side with a spear, and at once came out blood and water. He who saw it has borne witness – his testimony is true, and he knows that he is telling the truth – that you also may believe. For these things took place that the Scripture might be fulfilled: "Not one of his bones will be broken." And again another Scripture says: "They will look on him whom they have pierced."

John 19: 31-7

Guides and Insiders

As every seasoned traveller knows, it is one thing to buy a map or a guidebook; quite another to find a good guide. A good guide knows the locale at first hand and can show you around. Good guides often know the local area as insiders and insiders bestow advantages that maps and guidebooks never can. They often have contacts. They can sometimes get you in to places that might otherwise be closed to you. They have an unmistakable air of familiarity with local people and places. People know them. They know people. They blend in. They *belong*. And they know innumerable things that guidebooks never do.

As insiders, good guides usually make very good eyewitnesses as well: mostly because they are alert to things that most eyewitnesses miss. An eyewitness often stands on the outside looking in but an insider, by definition, stands on the *inside*: looking out and usually all around as well. And insiders are usually receptive to subtleties and nuances that outsiders are often blind to, making them *more* than mere eyewitnesses. They see the signs and they know how to read them. If you want to know the meaning of things it is usually best to ask an insider. Outsiders can look. But insiders can really *see*. And they know things that outsiders never do.

John as Eyewitness and Insider

Earlier chapters of this book have drawn attention to the fact that the author of John's gospel seems to be an eyewitness to the events he describes. He appears to know things that only an eyewitness would. He knows names, he knows places, and he has an eye for incidental detail which sometimes enables him to fill in 'gaps' that the other gospels leave unfilled. As we have already seen, he seems very much at home with the topography of Jerusalem and the surrounding area, and in his recounting of key events in the life of Jesus such as the calling of the earliest disciples, Jesus' actions and words during the 'cleansing' of the Temple and the events immediately following the Feeding of the Five Thousand he gives the distinct impression that either he writes about what he himself saw or what others known to him saw and told him. If he wasn't always there he usually seems to have been *close*: either as a direct eyewitness or as a sometime companion to others who were.

This chapter will draw much more detailed attention to the role of John as eyewitness as it explores the events leading up to and during Jesus' crucifixion. What it will add is an additional recognition of John as *insider* too. Standing on the inside of the events he describes, it is as if he is able to open a door for his readers as well, bestowing on all of us the temporary privileges of access to and understanding of events that only insiders have. That John is able to do this may, in turn, offer some clues as to who he actually was. Right at the beginning of this book it was suggested that our quest to explore Jesus *as* the Temple might bestow additional 'spin offs' and that one of these might be a deeper understanding of John as well as Jesus. As the events he describes reach their shocking climax we will see John stepping out of the shadows and attaining ever sharper definition. By the end of this chapter we will have seen and understood Jesus ever more clearly but we will also have caught a fresh sight of the man standing behind him as well.

'I Have Made Known Your Name'

As ever in John the timing and location of events are crucial and the clock ticks ever louder as the end draws nigh. Jesus has shared a final, intimate, meal with his disciples. He has promised that their sorrow will turn to joy and he has prayed for them. At the end of his prayer – in the very last verse of chapter seventeen of John's gospel – there is yet another reference to a new intimacy between Jesus, his disciples – or friends, as he now calls them - and the Father. Jesus, his eyes on heaven, closes his prayer to God with the words "I have made known to them your name, and I will continue to make it known, that the love with which you have loved me may be in them, and I in them" (John 17: 26). And with this his prayer ends. The opening of the next episode finds the small band of Jesus and his friends in the garden across the brook Kidron, with his betrayer almost at hand.

It is tempting to join them and to begin to trace John's 'counting down' of Jesus' final hours in chapters eighteen and nineteen of his gospel at this stage. But to do so would be to miss something crucial contained at several points in Jesus' final, moving, prayer to his Father on behalf of his friends: something that points forward to a *function* of Jesus that John sees as being closely bound up with his death and to which he will return as events unfold. Several times in his final prayer in chapter seventeen of John's gospel Jesus uses a distinctive phrase that invites closer attention than it is often given. In verse six, for example, Jesus prays to his Father: "I have revealed your name to the people whom you gave me out of the world." Later, in verse eleven, Jesus prays: "I am no longer in the world, but they are in the world, and I am coming to you. Holy Father, keep them in your name, which you have given me, that they may be one, even as we are one." Then in verse twelve, immediately afterwards, Jesus prays: "While I was with them, I kept them in your name, which you have given me." And almost at the very end of the prayer, as we have already noted, Jesus, praying now for those who will believe because of the testimony of the disciples, says to his Father: "I made known to them your name, and I will continue to make it known, that the love with which you loved me may be in them, and I in them."

The repeated references to the 'name' of the Father, given by Him to Jesus and by Jesus to the disciples and, by extension, to those who will later believe because of their testimony, is interesting. What is its significance, if any? One possibility is that the notion of 'God's name' is being used here in ways that are commonly found in the Old Testament, and that John is making a clear and explicit reference to these. So, for example, in Psalm 54 where the psalmist writes "Save me, O God, by thy name", 'name' is being used to designate God's power (Psalm 54: 1). Again, where the writer of Proverbs writes that "The name of the Lord is a strong tower" (Proverbs 18:10) a similar reference is being made to God as a powerful protector. Read in this way, Jesus' entreaty to his Father to "keep them [the disciples] in your name" may be seen as a way of saying "keep them in [or by] your power." In a similar way, Jesus' claim to have made known his Father's name to his disciples might simply be another way of saying that he has revealed to them his Father's power.

There is, however, another way of reading the references to the Father's name in Jesus' prayer which is very much in keeping with what we have been examining in this book. For it may be that in his claim to have received and revealed his Father's name Jesus is claiming to be able to do – and to have done – something that only the High Priest could do, and that in this way John is showing him to be performing a function that only somebody who was intrinsically and crucially bound up with the Temple could perform.

Within Judaism there have historically been – and still are – restrictions regarding the pronouncing and writing of God's name. Even today, the word 'God' is frequently written as 'G-D' in recognition that it is a word too holy to be casually written in full. By the time of Jesus, other words to refer to God – such as 'Lord' – were commonly used: practices which also still exist today. If the word is not written or spoken it cannot be blasphemed - even in error - and in prohibiting or restricting its use this possibility is correspondingly lessened. However, at the time of Jesus and for two or three centuries before, one key exception to the prohibition concerning the speaking of God's name existed. On the Day of Atonement, when the High Priest went into the Holy of Holies to make atonement for the sins of the people – the only day of the year when the Law permitted him to do this – he pronounced the name of the Lord in the Temple and this is recorded in several places in the Talmud. At several points in *Mishnah Yoma* which preserves in detail what happened on the Day of Atonement we learn that the High Priest did this, and that '[W]hen the priests and the people who were standing in the courtyard [on the Day of Atonement] heard the fully pronounced name come from the mouth of the High Priest they would kneel, prostrate themselves, fall on their knees, and call out: "Blessed be the Name of His glorious kingdom for ever and ever."' (*Mishnah Yoma* 6:2). *Mishnah Yoma* also tells us that the High Priest mumbled this or merged it with the singing of the priests because of the increase in immorality, but that in previous times it could be heard as far as Jericho (in what sounds like a piece of deliberate exaggeration!). What seems clear is that by the time of Jesus the knowledge of and corresponding pronunciation of the Divine Name in the – perhaps muffled - hearing of the people was the prerogative of the High Priest alone, and that in claiming to know it and to have made it known Jesus is, in the prayer in John 17, claiming to be able to do what only the High Priest could do. In fact, he goes so far as to claim that he has received the name directly from his Father, when he says of the disciples that "I kept them in your name, which you have given me" (John 17: 12).

A Clock Ticking

We will have cause to return to the portrayal by John of Jesus as High Priest. It recurs at crucial points as the crucifixion happens and subsequent events unfold and John draws attention to it in his typically ingenious and creatively symbolic ways – ways with which we have now become familiar. His artistry and subtlety are very much in evidence as he describes the events leading up to the crucifixion too.

Although the unfolding events combine to present a picture ever more shocking and horrific, the beauty of the writing remains undimmed, even in the darkness of the garden across the brook Kidron. Here, at the beginning of chapter eighteen, John portrays Jesus and the disciples being approached by a band of Roman soldiers, some officers from the chief priests, and some Pharisees: with Judas leading the way. It is a more detailed description than any presented in the other three gospels and John tells us several things that Matthew, Mark and Luke do not. He alone tells us that Roman soldiers were a part of this group whose intent was to arrest Jesus. He alone tells us of the groups' falling to the ground when Jesus declares his identity. He alone tells us of the 'lanterns and torches': an ironic detail given that this feeble illumination is intended to help facilitate the arrest of the one who called himself the light of the world (John 18: 3). And he alone records an apparently incidental detail that we will have cause to return to later. For while all four gospels tell of a brief sword fight at the point of arrest, only John tells us the apparently inconsequential detail that the name of the High Priest's servant whose right ear was cut off was Malchus.

In fact, John continues to provide detail not found in the other three gospels in his depiction of the events following Jesus' arrest. He alone tells us that Annas was father-in-law to the High Priest Caiaphas and he alone tells us that Jesus was taken to the former for questioning after his arrest before being taken to the latter. And in his description of the events that occurred in the courtyard of the High Priest he presents another piece of apparently inconsequential detail that will be needful of more detailed examination later. He tells us that 'that disciple' who followed Jesus along with Peter was 'known to the High Priest': something that grants both him and Peter access to the courtyard (John 18: 16). Given that there is little doubt that the reference to 'that disciple' is a reference to John himself, it implies that he was somehow known to Caiaphas (and perhaps, by extension, to the High Priestly family too). In fact, the word that John uses for 'known to' – *gnostos* - is particularly interesting, given that it means more than a merely casual or 'nodding' acquaintance and, instead, implies a much closer kinship. In fact, it carries the meaning of *close* friend as in Psalm 55:13: "But it is you, a man, my equal, my companion, my *gnostos*, [which the ESV renders as 'familiar friend']." Given that we have already learned that John seems to know the name of the High Priest's servant, it should come as no surprise to learn that he is a familiar friend of the High Priest. Indeed, it begins to look very much as if John is in a crucial sense an insider within the High Priestly 'court'. That he is given apparently privileged access to the courtyard at the time of Jesus' questioning by Annas and Caiaphas simply adds to the suspicion that close familiarity exists between him and them. That John alone will shortly add the detail that the occasion of Peter's third denial of Jesus is a question from 'one of the High Priest's servants, a kinsman of the man whose ear Peter had cut off' strengthens the case for viewing him as an insider with 'insider knowledge' yet further (John 18: 26).

The Passover Lamb

From Annas and Caiaphas Jesus passes into the hands of Pilate and eventually, despite apparently great reluctance, Pilate passes the sentence of death. John tells us that Pilate handed Jesus over to be crucified on 'the day of preparation for the Passover [at] about the sixth hour.' (John 19: 14). This piece of detail is crucial to an understanding of what follows, given that it was the exact time that the lambs that were to be eaten during the Passover feast were being slaughtered by the priests in the Temple.

The origin of the Passover feast is found in the book of Exodus in a well-known passage that describes the events that immediately preceded the escape of the Israelites from Egypt. God had already sent nine plagues on Egypt, yet still Pharaoh did not let the people of Israel leave. Exodus 11: 10 tells us that 'the Lord hardened Pharaoh's heart, and he did not let the people of Israel go out of his land.' So God sends a tenth and final plague: the most devastating one of all. He tells Moses that "This month shall be for you the beginning of months. It shall be the first month of the year for you" (Exodus 12: 2). It seems that what will follow will not be the last in a series of events but the opening of a new chapter. And so it proves. God strikes down every one of the firstborn of Egypt with a devastating plague but the Israelites are spared and this proves to be the decisive action in the forcing of Pharaoh's hand. How, then, does God know who the Israelites are and thus who to spare? The answer is once again in a set of detailed instructions which He gives to Moses: instructions given prior to the deadly event which will ensure the survival of those firstborn sons whose families follow the instructions which God has given. He says: "Go and select lambs for yourselves according to your clans, and kill the Passover lamb. Take a bunch of hyssop and dip it in the blood that is in the basin, and touch the lintel and the doorposts with the blood that is in the basin. None of you shall go out of the door of his house until the morning. For the Lord will pass through to strike the Egyptians, and when he sees the blood on the lintel and on the two doorposts, the Lord will pass over the door and will not allow the destroyer to enter your houses to strike you" (Exodus 12: 21-3). These same lambs whose sprinkled blood will ensure the survival of the firstborn are themselves to be eaten, at night, roasted with unleavened bread and bitter herbs and in readiness for a speedy departure from Egypt. Nothing is to be allowed to remain until morning, for "on that very day" God will lead the people of Israel out of Egypt.

And thereafter, God says to Moses, the eating of the Passover lambs is to be a "rite as a statute…for ever." Henceforth the Passover is to be commemorated and celebrated every year, for Israel alone: "No foreigner or hired worker may eat of it. It shall be eaten in one house; you shall not take any of the flesh outside the house, and you shall not break any of its bones" (Exodus 12: 45-6).

That the handing over and crucifixion of Jesus is to be seen in this context is absolutely crucial, and John draws deliberate attention to it in his description of the exact time at which Pilate handed Jesus over. Typical of John, this is more than mere 'backdrop' or supplementary information: it is critical for an understanding of what follows, as we will see. Yet it needs to be held 'in tension' with another recognition also. We noted towards the beginning of this chapter that John is keen to show that in his High Priestly prayer Jesus is claiming to do what only the High Priest could do in declaring the name of God on the Day of Atonement. Now, in his depiction of the events surrounding Jesus' crucifixion, he will be keen to show the meaning and significance of his death in the light of what happened at Passover. We will need to keep firmly in mind the difference between the Day of Atonement and the Feast of Passover in what follows. We will also need to think carefully about what it could possibly be that links these two events.

Casting Lots

Throughout his depiction of the events at the foot of Jesus' cross John once again provides details that the other gospel writers do not and there is once again a strong suspicion that we are dealing with the testimony of somebody who was actually *there*. Only John, for example, has the detail of the soldiers casting lots for one, specified, garment: Jesus' tunic, which he would have worn as his inner garment. Mark simply tells us that '[T]hey crucified him and divided his garments among them, to decide what each should take' (Mark 15: 24). John, however, draws particular attention to the fact that it was one particular item they gambled for: a seamless undergarment, or *chiton*, and seemingly the only thing of any value that Jesus possessed. Divided between the quaternion of soldiers it would be worthless, and John tells us that they apparently recognised this and hence gambled for it:

> 'When the soldiers had crucified Jesus, they took his garments and divided them into four parts, one part for each soldier; also his tunic. But the tunic was seamless, woven in one piece from top to bottom, so they said to one another, "Let us not tear it, but cast lots for it to see whose it shall be." This was to fulfil the Scripture which says, "They divided my garments among them, and for my clothing cast lots"'(John 19: 23-4)

As ever in John it is possible to try to understand the significance of the seamless garment in a number of ways. Some have suggested, for example, that there is a symbolic significance to the robe's indivisibility and that it might point forward to the future 'unity' of the church. However, it may well be that there is a deeper significance than this to *both* the garment *and* the means by which the soldiers gambled for it: a significance in keeping with other things that John has been eager to draw attention to up to this point. John tells us that they decided to cast lots for it, and this would almost certainly have involved the rolling or casting of dice. Roman dice are well-represented in archaeological finds from the region, many being found to be made of bone and marked like our own, and it is clear that centurions would have used them in gambling games in Israel and elsewhere. But John uses a very interesting term here for 'cast lots' – *lagzano* – which in its usual Biblical sense is used to refer to the casting of lots that the priests performed in order to determine who would carry out certain duties in the Temple. It is the word that Luke uses, for example, when at the beginning of his gospel he refers to Zechariah who on the day that the angel spoke to him regarding the birth of his son John the Baptist was 'on duty' in the Temple having been 'chosen by lot to enter the Temple of the Lord and burn incense' in accordance with 'the custom of the priesthood' (Luke 1: 8-9). In fact, priests cast lots to determine the performing of various priestly Temple duties, including who would put the showbread on the table and who would light the candles. Given that John has an ongoing concern to show the centrality of the Temple – and meanings arising from this - to many key events in his gospel, it is tempting to see a similar concern in the recounting of this detail here, including the deliberate use of *lagzano*. Are the Romans being shown as carrying out a grotesque parody of a Temple duty as they sit and gamble at the feet of the one who claimed to *be* the Temple?

Woven From Above

The suspicion that the episode is being deliberately portrayed to evoke thoughts of Jesus as in some sense embodying the Temple in his own person is further reinforced when another word which John uses to describe an aspect of this scene is considered. It is one that is often mistranslated and the significance of it is not always grasped. In verse 23 of chapter nineteen of his gospel John describes the garment for which the soldiers gambled as not only 'seamless' but 'woven in one piece from top to bottom' and the word he uses to describe this apparent direction of the weave is in fact *anothen*, which literally means 'from above'. It is found elsewhere in his gospel, for example in the episode in which Nicodemus comes to Jesus by night to be told that unless he is 'born again' he cannot see the Kingdom of God. The actual word that John uses for 'again' is *anothen*, which changes the meaning of Jesus' statement significantly, transforming it into an admonition to Nicodemus that he must be born "from above" if he wishes to see – or enter into - the Kingdom. It is not at all clear why *anothen* is usually translated as 'again' in the Nicodemus 'encounter': 'from above' is clearly the more accurate rendering (John 3: 3).

Assuming that as with *lagzano* the use of the word *anothen* is deliberate and given the way that John has used the word previously we may reasonably conclude that more is being revealed in John's use of it in his distinctive telling of the gambling incident than the mere direction in which the *chiton* was woven. That the garment was woven 'from above' at least *suggests* that it was God who had, in fact, woven it, and that John is trying to show that Jesus' garment had been somehow 'made for' him by his Father above.

This would be an admittedly tenuous suggestion but for the fact that a seamless garment woven in one piece was a distinctive part of the High Priest's clothing. The origin of this can be traced back to God's instructions to Moses at Mount Sinai where He made clear exactly how the priests and High Priest should be dressed. Thus, we read in Exodus 28: 31-2 that "You shall make the robe of the *ephod* all of blue. It shall have an opening for the head in the middle of it, with a woven binding round the opening, like the opening in a garment, so that it may not tear." The "so that it may not tear" is closely reminiscent of the soldiers' stated reluctance to tear Jesus' robe - and which led to their casting lots for it - and when we recall to mind that John has previously shown how Jesus, in making the Father's name known, has already performed a High Priestly action, the significance of his robe being associated with that of the High Priest's *ephod* becomes more readily apparent. That in the case of Jesus his robe has been woven 'from above' suggests that he is being portrayed as a High Priest dressed specifically by his Father and this clothing of him in this special way may also be seen as reminiscent of Jesus' claim in John chapter ten verse 36 to be "him whom the Father consecrated and sent out into the world." That John has thus portrayed Jesus by this point as both High Priest *and* Temple is entirely in keeping with what we have seen to be his consistent portrayal of Jesus in his gospel.

Blood and Water

Yet John has still to deliver an even bolder and more striking allusion to Jesus as the embodiment of the Temple. And side by side with his portrayal of Jesus as High Priest he does not forget the significance of the Passover Festival for another understanding of Jesus also: that of the Passover lamb. Thus, when a branch of hyssop is dipped into sour wine to slake Jesus' thirst, the use of hyssop in the sprinkling of the blood of the Passover lamb in the Exodus story is readily recalled to mind (John 19: 29). And when the episode is recounted by John of the soldiers deciding not to break Jesus' legs – because he has already died - the association of this with God's instruction to Moses that the bones of the Passover lamb were not to be broken is an additional link easily made (John 19: 33). In fact, there does not seem to be a great deal of subtlety here. Anybody familiar with the detail of the Passover narratives in the Hebrew Scriptures would make the connection and both the timing and the detail of John's crucifixion account seem to actively invite it. It is scarcely believable that John is unaware of the link. Although we have yet to consider how Jesus can be both High Priest and sacrifice at the same time it is apparent that John *is* showing him to be both. Yet, remarkable as it may seem, even *this* is almost incidental in the light of what is to follow.

Immediately after his description of how the soldiers did not break Jesus' legs, John tells us what one of them did instead. He writes that 'one of the soldiers pierced his side with a spear, and at once there came out blood and water' (John 19: 34). Then we read the narrator's commentary on this piece of detail: 'He who saw it has borne witness – his testimony is true, and he knows that he is telling the truth – that you also may believe' (John 19: 35). We will take each of these sentences in turn.

The blood and water flowing from Jesus' pierced side is a detail of John's gospel that has long fascinated commentators and casual readers alike. Once again, it is a detail that only John gives. The fact that people were crucified relatively close to the ground – and not high up on the top of tall wooden crosses as in some Christian art – means that an eye-witness at the foot of the cross would see it clearly. That it was later seen to be a detail occasioning special note – perhaps even

108

surprise – is apparent from the line that follows which draws attention to the reliability and truthfulness of the witness. What, then, might it mean, and why might it be so important?

As with the undivided undergarment, the flow of blood and water can be viewed symbolically as relating to the church that was to follow the death and resurrection of its 'founder': and so it has been. Seen in this way, the blood and water have been seen to symbolise the sacraments of baptism and communion, for example. Another frequently-encountered suggestion is that John was trying to make clear via this piece of detail that Jesus, having been fully a man, had now completely died – thus refuting later claims within the early years of the church and elsewhere that Jesus had not been fully human or had not been really dead. As interesting as these interpretations are, a third interpretation can be considered at this point, and once again the backdrop and context of the Passover are important.

One census taken shortly after Jesus' lifetime and conducted by one Cestius to show to Emperor Nero the importance of Jerusalem suggests that approximately 256,000 lambs were slaughtered by the priests during the time of preparation for the Passover. Whilst this figure is contested it is undeniably the case that lambs were slaughtered in vast numbers during the festival: in their tens of thousands at least. The altar and the area around it must have been literally awash with blood from so many sacrifices being made during such a relatively short period. And this raises the question: where did all the blood actually *go*? It must have run like a river from the place of sacrifice during times like Passover. How then, did they get rid of it?

Once again we turn to later Jewish writings that have preserved Temple practices that existed at the time of Jesus. In the *Mishnah* we read something interesting about the altar on which sacrifices were slaughtered. It refers to the altar itself: 'At the south-western corner there were two holes like two narrow nostrils by which the blood that was poured over the western base and the southern base used to run down and mingle in the water channel and flow out into the brook Kidron (*Mishnah: m.Middot* 3:2). This seems to have been how they got rid of the blood. It drained through two holes in the south-western corner of the altar. Water flowed underneath. The blood mixed with the water and drained out from the Temple and into the brook that ran away from the Temple and into the Kidron Valley. It was a form of drainage which used existing water flow to wash the blood out and away from the Temple.

Might this explain the particular interest of John in the blood and water flowing from Jesus' side? Clearly, blood mixed with water flowed from the place of sacrifice in the Temple: at some times – such as Passover - in significantly greater volume than at others. And standing at the foot of the cross, John sees the same mixed flow now running away from Jesus. That this at the very least serves yet again to reinforce his identification of Jesus with the Temple seems clear. John has previously shown him to be the Tabernacling presence, the meeting-place of heaven and earth, an embodied Temple that will be raised in the wake of its destruction, a 'new' and future Temple from which life-giving waters will flow, the 'belly' from which believers are invited to drink, a Temple directly consecrated from his Father in Heaven, a High Priest with a garment woven from 'above', and a sacrifice being made at the exact time that the Passover lambs were being slaughtered. Now it is as if John is showing him to be the *place* of sacrifice too: a place from which blood and water flows, as it did from the Temple altar. Anybody who knew how the blood was washed away from the Temple when sacrifice was made would surely make the connection: particularly, perhaps, somebody who was an 'insider' to the priesthood and who might consequently have had thoughts of Temple practice uppermost in his mind.

'He Who Saw It Has Borne Witness'

The writer of John's gospel intrudes frequently into the narrative, as we have seen. He clarifies Jewish concepts and practices unfamiliar to Jewish readers. He supplies incidental detail such as times and places. He corrects statements that he knows to be incorrect. He supplies context. And so on. Yet the intrusion here is particularly striking. He interrupts the flow of the narrative at the very point at which attention is drawn to the blood and water flowing from Jesus' side to draw the reader's attention to the trustworthiness of the witness in a way that has not happened up to this point in the gospel, despite the frequency of prior 'intrusions'. 'He who saw it has borne witness,' claims the gospel, 'his testimony is true, and he knows he is telling the truth – that you also may believe.' It is as if this particular piece of detail is so important that the reader must be assured that it can actually be traced back to a witness that can be trusted. But why? After all, it is not the most miraculous thing that has occurred. By now, the reader of John's gospel has read of bread and wine being extraordinarily multiplied, the lame walking, the blind seeing, and a dead man being raised, amongst other remarkable things. No attempt has been made to 'vouch' for the trustworthiness of the 'source' in these instances. Why now, unless the claim that is being made has a special significance and is one on which so much else rests? Could that claim be that Jesus *is* the Temple, that the dramatic flow from his body 'crowns' and clinches this assertion, and that it is so important that the reader must be assured that it actually happened?

The Source of the Stream

Interestingly, this particular episode links back very closely to something that we have already encountered, but in a way that is so subtle – even prescient - that it almost beggars belief. Previously in this book we have seen how on the last and greatest day of the Feast of Tabernacles Jesus cried out that anybody who was thirsty should come to him and drink: specifically, from his navel, out of which he declared that rivers of living water would flow. We saw then that it was most likely that this was yet another claim to be the Temple and one which matched closely certain aspects of John's description of Jesus' encounter with the Samaritan woman earlier in the gospel. There, it will be recalled, we also noted that the 'belly' – or *omphalos* – as the source of the water was equated with the belief within Judaism and elsewhere that the Temple was the source or centre of creation: it's navel, in other words. At *this* point in John, we can 'step back' and consider a potential additional significance of the source of this new Temple's life-giving water being the belly.

A Physician's View

It is little surprise to learn that the detail of the crucifixion as given by John and the other gospel writers has been pored over by specialists in many fields. Not least amongst these have been doctors and other medical experts keen to compare the New Testament's description of events with what might be expected to occur medically to a man dying of crucifixion. We know, for example, that breaking bones to hasten death in crucifixion works because the unnatural posture of a person nailed to a cross requires them to breathe by pressing down on the legs. The breaking of the legs halts this painful and laboured process, bringing asphyxiation and instant death. Thus, the notion that centurions might break the legs of crucifixion victims to hasten their death and thereby ensure that they are able to be taken down from the cross by nightfall – a detail given in John – has been shown to be historically extremely probable. It also reinforces yet again the contention that the writer of John's gospel had witnessed crucifixions before and very probably the crucifixion of Jesus as well; knowing, as he does, that the breaking of the legs was the Roman practice in cases like this.

Some medical experts have gone as far as to attempt reconstructed *autopsies* based on the detail given in the gospels and John has been particularly useful to them in this regard, given the amount of detail he provides. After all, Jesus was dead when the blood and water flowed. What, then, can be inferred from this? One interesting attempt to account for the flow has proceeded like this: a Roman soldier is trained. He knows that a thrust through the left-hand side of the chest a little below the centre will penetrate both the heart and the lung. The thrust will – when made from below – enter the left-hand side of the upper abdomen, opening Jesus' already swollen stomach. It will pierce the diaphragm, cut wide open the heart with its vessels and arteries and lacerate the lung. This will cause a large wound: one large enough to thrust a hand into. Blood from the veins and dilated right side of the heart will mix with water from the stomach. Hence the flow of water and blood seen in such detail by John from below.

For one thing, such a reconstruction shows how plausible it is that blood mixed with water would flow from a newly-crucified man, vindicating John as a reliable source of what he reports once again. More importantly, however, it draws attention to the fact that whilst the blood would flow from the area in and around the heart, the water would flow from the *stomach*. That this is consistent with the notion of water flowing from Jesus' belly already encountered in John is striking. Was Jesus making a veiled allusion to the manner of his own death – and an event that was immediately to follow it – as early as the Feast of Tabernacles? Could John have known this when he wrote his gospel? These questions cannot, of course, be answered with any degree of certainty and it is possible to account for the blood-and-water flow in other ways, such as that the water was not water in the strict sense but pericardial fluid. But the flowing of water from the belly which *potentially* links these two separate occasions remains very possible and would be remarkable indeed, particularly when it is borne in mind that, as we have been seeing, there are few – if any – 'mere coincidences' in John.

A Priestly Insider

This has been a long chapter because John has a lot to say about the crucifixion and its ultimate and overall meaning. And it has become clear as we close that John – or the source upon which John's gospel draws - is a character in the drama he unfolds, apparently allowing him to give us a wealth of 'eye witness' detail that the other gospels do not and adding confirmatory detail of what that gospel itself tells us: that the eyewitness to the events that it relates was at the foot of the cross and so close to Jesus that he could hear what was said to him by Jesus about taking Mary into his own home as her 'son'. What has become equally clear is that much of the detail that John's gospel provides suggests a closeness to the Temple and its priesthood either on the part of its writer or that writer's 'close up' source. As we have seen, only John's gospel gives us the name of the High Priest's servant whose ear Peter cut off. Only John tells us that the disciple who accompanied Peter to the High Priest's courtyard – apparently John himself - was a *gnostos* to the High Priest in a way suggesting closeness rather than formal familiarity and that this was how he gained admission to the High Priest's courtyard for himself and Peter. John even tells us that the 'trigger' for Peter's third denial of Jesus is a question from a relative of the High Priest's servant whose ear Peter struck: he can be *that* specific.

And throughout, John's gospel has a concern to set out detail and the *meaning* of that detail which suggests that the writer is looking at events with what we might call a 'priestly eye'. This is particularly the case in that gospel's description of the events around the cross, where the writer uses a Temple phrase for 'casting lots' in his description of the game the soldiers played for Jesus' *chiton*: a garment which itself is suggestive of the High Priest's *ephod*. And the timing and detail of the crucifixion events themselves suggests very strongly that the writer is deliberately portraying Jesus as the Passover lamb being prepared and slain at the very time that the Passover lambs were being prepared and slain in the Temple. That he adds a description of the flow of blood and water from Jesus' side in terms once again suggestive of what happened in and around the Temple at Passover suggests that the source that stands behind John's gospel is what we might call a 'priestly insider': somebody who is viewing events as such an insider would. This has been a clear conclusion that this chapter has drawn and it provides a powerful clue as to who the author of John's gospel actually was: one which we will have cause to return to and develop in future chapters.

A New Temple

What has become very clear also is that, for John, Jesus is the Passover lamb. It is as if he is saying: 'The meaning of Passover has reached its climax, or fulfilment, or deepest meaning, in the crucifixion of Jesus.' Hence the timing and detail of the events he sets out. In the previous chapter we saw how Jesus is portrayed by John as the 'real' or 'true' vine: and hence in yet another crucial sense as the 'real' or 'true' Temple. A similar concern appears to be at work in John's portrayal of the crucifixion also. It is as if he is saying: 'You have sacrificed Passover lambs for centuries. But Jesus is the *real* Passover lamb. In this way and in this respect he is yet again to be seen in terms of being a new Temple.' It is a striking claim: one not always entirely understood and one certainly not without its problems.

One misunderstanding of the claim could take – and has typically taken - the following form: Jesus is the *real* Passover lamb, hence he is the *real* sacrifice for sins. What had previously happened in the Temple as a means toward securing the forgiveness of sins is henceforth obsolete because a new 'means' or 'mechanism' has taken its place. The new has taken the place of the old and henceforth forgiveness of sins can be seen as having been accomplished thanks to a 'new' or 'everlasting' Passover sacrifice. The problem here is that the Passover sacrifice was never viewed as the means by which forgiveness of sins was achieved and was never celebrated as such. In fact, Jews had - and have - an entirely different event in their calendar to celebrate and commemorate this: the Day of Atonement, an event entirely separate to Passover, taking place at an entirely different time of year. That was the case in Jesus' day, just as it is now.

So what *did* Passover mean when John wrote his gospel? What would it have meant to Jesus? It would appear from various sources, including the *Mishnah*'s Tractate *Pesahim*, that Passover - then and subsequently - meant several things and what they all had in common was deliverance from one condition into a better one: as was the case when the final plague led to the Israelites' escape from Egyptian bondage and captivity. So, at Passover, Jews remembered – and still remember – how they were delivered out of bondage and into freedom, out of sorrow into gladness, out of mourning and into festivity, out from darkness and into great light, and out of servitude and into redemption. Indeed, something of this transformation of one state into a better state may be grasped from John's description of Jesus' promise to the disciples shortly before his final prayer for them: "A little while, and you will see me no longer; and again a little while, and you will see me...Truly, truly, I say to you, you will weep and lament, but the world will rejoice. You will be sorrowful, but your sorrow will turn into joy" (John 16: 16 – 20). That this is an accurate portrayal of sorrow turning into gladness and mourning turning into festivity reflects precisely what it was that Passover would have meant to the disciples to whom the promise was made. That Passover also recalled to mind the transition from servitude to redemption might also be reflected in

Jesus' calling of his disciples 'friends' rather than 'servants' on the same occasion (John 15: 14-15).

This recognition of what it really means to see Jesus as the Passover sacrifice – and what, by extension, it does *not* mean – raises another, crucial, question: if Jesus is *not* being portrayed by John as atoning for sin in his death as Passover lamb, where exactly *is* he shown to be the one through whom atonement is made? There is no doubt that John *does* see Jesus as the one through whom atonement is secured and sins forgiven. But if he does *not* do this in his portrayal of Jesus' crucifixion, where *does* he do it? This will be the central question that the next chapter will be concerned to answer.

Chapter Eight: Strips of Linen

Now on the first day of the week Mary Magdalene came to the tomb early, while it was still dark, and saw that the stone had been taken away from the tomb. So she ran and went to Simon Peter and the other disciple, the one whom Jesus loved, and said to them, "They have taken the Lord out of the tomb, and we do not know where they have laid him." So Peter went out with the other disciple, and they were going towards the tomb. Both of them were running together, but the other disciple outran Peter and reached the tomb first. And stooping to look in, he saw the linen cloths lying there, but he did not go in. Then Simon Peter came, following him, and went into the tomb. He saw the linen cloths lying there, and the face cloth, which had been on Jesus' head, not lying with the linen cloths but in a place by itself. Then the other disciple, who had reached the tomb first, also went in, and he saw and believed; for as yet they did not understand the Scripture that he must rise from the dead. Then the disciples went back to their homes.

But Mary stood weeping outside the tomb, and as she wept she stooped to look into the tomb. And she saw two angels in white, sitting where the body of Jesus had lain, one at the head and one at the feet.

John 20: 1 - 12

Defilement and Death

It is remarkable to think that the sheer fact of death and decay could dictate the layout of a city and its surrounding area. But this has been the case, historically, with Jerusalem, as many recent and not-so-recent archaeological finds have shown. We now know that by the time of Jesus there were numerous tombs within the Jerusalem area although not in the city itself – with the exception of the tombs of the House of

David and the Prophetess Hulda. Burial in trenches or simple earth graves appears to have been very rare, but rock tombs in which the dead were laid have been found in large numbers in clustered areas around the city although no tombs within *any* area have been found to the west of the Temple, despite numerous (and ongoing) archaeological discoveries of burial sites dating back to – and before – the time of Jesus. The reason for this uneven geographical distribution appears initially obscure but turns out to be relatively simple, given the way that death and decay were (and are) seen as potent sources of defilement according to the Jewish law. The prevailing winds blow from the west. Thus, if tombs were located to the west of the city there was the possibility that the winds would blow impurity and decay east across the city and into its most sacred precincts: including, of course, those of the Temple. Hence no tombs were located in any area west of the Temple in order to exclude any possibility of defilement in this way.

Death defiled, as did contact with the dead. Hence precautions were taken to exclude every possibility of defilement caused by contact with death. Tombs were even whitewashed to prevent them from being stumbled over accidentally after dark, and this fact provides the context for the understanding of Jesus' denunciation of the Pharisees as "whitewashed tombs, which outwardly appear beautiful, but within are full of dead people's bones and uncleanness." (Matthew 23: 27). Not only would this have been a shocking denunciation, it also underlines the sense of corruption and uncleanness that death was seen to carry. A whitewashed tomb could indeed appear beautiful on the outside, but on the inside it was a very different story.

John tells us that the tomb in which Joseph of Arimathea and Nicodemus laid Jesus was 'in the place where he was crucified [where] there was a garden, and in the garden a new tomb in which no one had yet been laid' (John 19: 41). The precision of the location and the detail of its description are not unexpected: as we have had abundant cause to note, the author of John's gospel knows Jerusalem. And as we have had equally abundant cause to note, time as well as location are important to him. In fact, time seems to be very much to the fore as we consider his description of the burial of Jesus and it seems to have dictated the choice of the tomb into which Jesus' lifeless body was placed. John asserts that Joseph of Arimathea and Nicodemus laid Jesus where they did because it was close at hand and it was the Jewish day of Preparation for the Passover. The body could not be allowed to be left on the cross at such a time – another instance of death defiling – and it therefore needed to be taken down, wrapped and anointed for burial, and buried. And it needed to be done quickly, as the end of day was fast approaching. How convenient and practical, then, that a new tomb was available close to the place of crucifixion into which Jesus' corpse could be placed. John tells us that Joseph of Arimathea secured permission from Pilate to take the body and that together with Nicodemus – and an apparently vast amount of myrrh and aloes – he took it, wrapped it in strips of linen 'in accordance with Jewish burial customs' and laid it in the tomb. With this, both Joseph and Nicodemus disappear from the gospel (John 19: 38-42).

According to Custom

In the normal course of events the body of a dead person would have been interred within a tomb in a long niche known as a *kokh*. This was basically a shelf cut into the tomb's wall about 1.2m from its floor and with a length of approximately 2m. There is no reason to doubt that this was done on the occasion of Jesus' own burial and that the Romans allowed Jewish persons to bury their dead according to their own law during times of peace is well-attested. There was no coffin and the niches – *kokhim* – were stone benches cut into the wall upon which the body was placed. Many of these were arched, although given that Jesus was put into a new tomb it is not clear that this degree of elaboration existed in the case of his particular burial place. He may well have been placed on a simple, bare, unelaborated, stone shelf. In many tombs the floor was excavated and deepened to create a sort of 'standing pit' in order to permit standing whilst the body was attended to, making the continuation of the process of wrapping and anointing easier. In a normal tomb there would have been three *kokhim*, one in each wall of a square tomb which was literally cut out of the rock: a process which would subsequently have been continued in order to expand and extend the tomb as generations lived and died and fresh need arose. The fourth wall would have contained no niche, given that it contained the entrance, which was cut into the rock at floor level and was sealable with a stone. You would need to stoop to see into or enter the tomb – in fact you would have to enter feet first or on your hands and knees - and once inside you would be able to arrange the body for its final resting place from a relatively comfortable standing position. Given that tombs were expanded as required and that, according to John, Jesus' tomb was a new one, it has been suggested that there was only one niche in his, although it is uncertain as to which wall it was cut into. Immediately outside the tomb was a 'forecourt' where some aspects of the preparation of the body could be carried out and where mourners could gather. Overall, it should be envisioned that the overall tomb layout was of a larger forecourt separated from the smaller, square, 'tomb proper' which was accessible via an entrance sealed with a stone. There was, thus, a 'large part' and a 'small part' to the kind of tomb into which Jesus was placed: a large 'communal' area for mourning - containing benches and washing basins for preparation of the body - being separated from the smaller, square, 'tomb proper' by a stone which would be rolled into place as a seal once the burial was completed.

Wrapping the Dead

As the description of the raising of Lazarus earlier in John's gospel makes clear, the body was wrapped in strips of linen but the head was wrapped in a separate cloth. It was not unknown for bodies to revive in the coolness of the tomb and hence a separate face cloth – or *soudarion* – wrapped the head. In the very unlikely event that the buried person was not actually dead and resuscitation occurred it could easily be blown off without the use of the hands, which were bound inside the strips of linen on either side of the body and not – as with Western burial - crossed in front of the genitals. Accurately reflecting this distinctive Jewish way of burying the dead, John tells us in his description of the raising of Lazarus that 'The man who had died came out, his hands and feet bound with linen strips, and his face wrapped with a cloth' (John 11: 44). This very particular way of wrapping the dead is something else that will become important to us later, although it is worth noting in passing at this point how it makes the Shroud of

Turin extremely unlikely to be the actual burial cloth of Jesus. As is widely-known, this large length of linen carries an image said to have been created when Jesus was raised from the dead. Complete with an image of the front and back of an apparently crucified man and including blood stains which appear to originate from the head, side, wrists, and ankles, it has long been an artefact of considerable controversy and has been the subject of repeated tests, including pollen analyses and carbon-14 dating. John shows us that it almost certainly cannot be authentic by making clear how the Jewish dead of Jesus' day were wrapped in strips of linen with an entirely separate 'head piece'. This is utterly different to the linen imprint on the Shroud of Turin in which the head and body are both represented on a single sheet which seems to have wrapped the whole body, front and back, from top to bottom. That the hands on the Shroud image are crossed over the genitals – and not placed to the sides of the body, as was the case with Jewish custom – casts further doubt on its authenticity as the actual burial shroud of Jesus.

A Tomb and a Twist

During Jesus' day, once a body had decayed sufficiently it was removed from its wrappings and the bones placed in an ossuary made of stone or wood. Tombs contained recesses for the containment of ossuaries, and many of these figure in archaeological finds from the region. Had Jesus' body remained in the tomb for this length of time – anywhere between twelve months and three years, given the climate of the area - his wrappings would have been removed after an appropriate length of time and his bones placed into a marked ossuary in accordance with Jewish custom. This would, of course, have necessitated a return to the Tomb and the removal of the stone in order to gain entrance to it.

However, readings of the Jewish law by the time of Jesus permitted a return to a deceased person's tomb much earlier than this. Indeed, such was encouraged. According to *Mishnah Semahot* 8:1, one should 'go to the cemetery to check the dead within three days, and not fear that such smacks of pagan practices.' As partial justification of this, it adds:

'There was actually one buried man who was visited after three days and lived for 25 more years and had sons, and died afterwards.' Whilst Matthew, Mark and Luke tell us that the occasion of the discovery that Jesus' tomb was empty was a visit from several women intending to anoint the body with spices, John tells us no such thing. According to his gospel, as we have seen, the anointing had already been done on the Day of Preparation by Joseph of Arimathea and Nicodemus. In fact, as we will see, the logic of his narrative – together with the meaning that the reader is intended to infer from it – demands that the anointing of the body with spices and strips of linen had occurred in advance of Mary's visit and thus dictates that her visit could not therefore have been to anoint and wrap the body.

Why *would* she have been visiting the tomb, then? Might it have been to check on the state of the deceased in accordance with what the Law permitted; an occasion which presented a further opportunity for mourning? John tells us that she came 'early, while it was still dark' but that far from finding a dead body she initially found that the stone had been removed. Her reaction at this point is to run to tell others. Finding Peter 'and the other disciple, the one whom Jesus loved', she breathlessly informs them that the body has been taken (John 20: 1-2). It is generally supposed that the disciple that was with Peter, 'the one whom Jesus loved', was none other than John (or John's source), and this is supported by the detailed narrative detail that the gospel gives in what follows.

Indeed, and throughout, it smacks of *reportage*, once again reinforcing the suspicion that the source for it is somebody who was actually there. John's gospel tells us that having received Mary's report the two disciples set off at a run. Having started together, however, the other disciple outruns Peter, reaching the tomb first. As John tells the story: 'And stooping to look in, he saw the linen cloths lying there, but he did not go in. Then Simon Peter came, following him, and went into the tomb. He saw the linen cloths lying there, and the face cloth, which had been on Jesus' head, not lying with the linen cloths but folded up in a place by itself. Then the other disciple, who had reached the tomb first, also went in, and he saw and believed; for as yet they did not understand the Scripture, that he must rise from the dead' (John 20: 5-10).

As ever, John says much here with few words, and the full meaning lies below an apparently straightforward surface. That the other disciple outruns Peter suggests that he is the younger man, able to run faster. But it is notable that having reached the tomb first, he does not go in first. Instead, he waits for Peter. Why? A common view is that Peter was the acknowledged leader of the disciples and the other disciple's hesitation reflects his deference in view of this fact. This is certainly plausible, and the picture of Peter we get from all four gospels as an impulsive – even, on occasion, rash – individual allows us to easily imagine him plunging into the darkness of a tomb where the other man has hesitated, perhaps deferentially but perhaps out of some fear also. This book's recognition of the source behind John's gospel as a 'priestly insider', however, suggests another view. If the source *was* such a person, it is, of course, quite possible that he was actually a serving priest with priestly duties which contact with the dead would forbid him from performing until he was restored to ritual purity again. If such was the case, we can well understand his waiting for Peter. It is not mere deference, nor fear, but a concern as a priest to remain ritually pure in order to avoid the carrying out of a detailed process which would be needed for him to resume his duties again. So he waits until Peter arrives and gives him the 'all clear' – "There's nobody here!", or some such first-century Aramaic equivalent – before he, too, enters the tomb.

Strips of Linen

The sight that initially greets Peter, and then the other disciple, is at first a puzzling one. Most obviously, however, Mary's earlier breathless message appears confirmed: at least initially. The other disciple can see the strips of linen lying on the ground before he even enters. But it is dark and day has barely dawned. Is the body in there or not? Then Peter arrives and goes in. He sees more: the linen that should have been wrapped around Jesus' body is there on its own and apart from the facecloth, which seems to have been removed with some deliberation, folded, and put in a place by itself: perhaps in the niche where the body should have lain. This additional detail confirms Mary's message: there is no body here at all and Jesus must have therefore been taken away, his location unknown. Untroubled by any danger of ritual impurity, the other disciple can now enter. He sees what Peter sees but John's gospel tells us that he both saw *and believed*. It is as if John is trying to tell us that at this point, for that disciple, the one whom Jesus loved, the 'penny drops'. He gets it. But what does he 'get'?

Firstly and most obviously, he appears to 'get' the fact that Jesus has in some sense risen from the dead. John's gospel appears to underline this by stating that up to this point – 'as yet' – they did not understand the scripture, but the sight of the grave clothes lying empty suddenly opens that disciple's eyes to a fact that Jesus has previously tried to make clear on many occasions: that he will die but then rise.

This has been a traditional understanding of the significance of the sight of the grave clothes and one which is followed by many commentators. But is this all there is to it? The arrangement of the grave clothes – described with such precision in John's gospel – has certainly been the occasion of much scholarly discussion. It appears to be very important to John to tell us exactly how the grave clothes are arranged and he goes to great length to do so, describing the linen cloths – first from the other disciple's perspective and then Peter's – and then the position and arrangement of the head cloth, including the additional detail that this had been folded up. This arrangement of the body and face wrappings could convey several things, and these have been commonly noted. Firstly, it seems to preclude the possibility that the body had been stolen, perhaps by grave robbers. Given the urgency with which they would have had to do their 'work', it has been argued that grave robbers would not have gone to the trouble of removing the wrappings and folding some of them before removing the body from the tomb. Rather, in their urgency, they would simply have bundled up the body, grave clothes and all, and taken it out of the tomb as it was. That this was not done suggests that the body was not stolen. Or even moved for the purposes of relocating the body. In either case, the wrappings would have been left on the corpse. This is a plausible interpretation of the situation that greeted the other disciple and Peter: that whatever else might have happened, they were certainly not dealing with the theft or simple moving of Jesus' body.

Another possibility is that the separate location of the body wrappings and the head wrapping is evidence that the resurrected body simply rose through and out of the grave clothes: that it 'dematerialized' as it passed through them *en route* to its newly-resurrected state. This has also been a popular view and whilst it is imaginative – and even exciting – it seems clear from what we have so far noted that it fails to do justice to what John has been at pains to tell us: that the head piece had been *folded up and placed with some deliberation* where Peter and the other disciple found it. We would certainly not expect that observation if the body had miraculously 'passed through' the wrappings, leaving them behind. In such a scenario the head piece would surely appear discarded, not folded. But John has been at pains to tell us that it *was* folded, as we have already noted.

This folding has received comparatively less attention from commentators than the simple arrangement of the linen, but attempts have been made to explain it in terms of what a carpenter would do when he finished a job – he would fold up a cloth – or what a rabbi would do to express his displeasure at a meal that had failed to satisfy him. Once again these are imaginative, even ingenious, attempts to explain the folding, but neither is really suggested by the context in which the arrangement of the grave clothes occurs in John: in the empty tomb of the now-missing Jesus.

Yom Kippur

Let us, then, reframe the questions that the apparently deliberate arranging of the grave clothes presents and try to answer them within the context of this book's attempt to understand John's presentation of Jesus as the Temple. Say it was Jesus himself who removed his *own* grave clothes. Why would he do it with such deliberation? Why fold the head wrapping: perhaps placing it on the tomb's now bodiless niche? Is this, perhaps, a deliberate attempt to remind somebody of something? Might that 'something' have been of such importance to the writer or source of John's gospel that he was at pains to draw the reader's attention to it too? And might the shock of understanding this particular arrangement of burial clothes have been the cause of the other disciples' seeing *and* believing? Might it even provide a clue as to *what* it was he believed: something, perhaps, in *addition* to the fact that Jesus had risen from death?

Atonement for Sin

In the last chapter we saw how John presents Jesus' death in terms suggestive of the sacrifice of a perfect Passover lamb. But we also noted that another *motif* seems to intrude on this. In addition to being the sacrifice, John appears to be trying to show that Jesus was in some sense the High Priest too; at least, this is suggested by the detail that he gives of the gambling for Jesus' one-piece tunic of the kind that the High Priest would have worn and by his previous presentation of Jesus who, like the High Priest on the Day of Atonement, makes known God's name. Sacrifice *and* High Priest? It is a puzzle, and yet it is one that provides opportunities for the solving of other puzzles too. In particular, we have seen how, whilst the Passover sacrifice meant many things, it was not seen in terms of the making of atonement for sin. This was something that required a very elaborate ritual of its own; one which required the detailed participation of the High Priest. This festival – the Day of Atonement or Yom Kippur – has its roots in the history of the people of Israel and, like all of the major Jewish festivals, is given detailed description in the Old Testament: specifically, in the Torah. And, as we will now see, it provides a powerful clue as to what the apparently deliberate arrangement of the grave clothes meant to the disciple who saw *and* believed.

The Day of Atonement was the one occasion in the entire Jewish calendar when anyone was allowed to go into the Temple's Holy of Holies, and even then it was only the High Priest that was allowed to enter. But he had to take great care before doing so. Such was the holiness of this place that he had to do everything exactly as the Law prescribed, including making sure he was dressed appropriately. Leviticus 16 gives very detailed instructions as to how Aaron, the first High Priest, was to conduct himself on this occasion, and makes clear that in future generations Aaron's High Priestly successors must perform it as a 'permanent law' in order to make atonement annually on this special day. In other words, future High Priests had to follow in Aaron's footsteps and prepare and conduct themselves on the Day of Atonement as Aaron himself had been instructed to do.

Thus, the Law laid down for all successive generations of High Priests that they first of all had to prepare themselves carefully for this complex ritual. In fact, the Day of Atonement was to be comprised of a complex *series* of rituals including the burning of incense, the morning sacrifice, additional sacrifices and the drawing of stones from an urn to determine which of two goats was for sacrifice and which would be released into the wilderness carrying away with it the sins of the people. This, in fact, is the origin of the word 'scapegoat': a word which shorn of its original ritual associations is still found in popular usage. The sacrifice of a bullock after the drawing of stones was of particular importance, given that it was an atonement for the sins of the High Priest himself together with his family. The sacrifice of the other goat was also important as a cleansing from sin of the Temple/Tabernacle including its holiest place, the Holy of Holies. And the release of the scapegoat into the wilderness provided the means for the transferral of the people's sins onto an animal which would carry those sins far away. All told, done correctly, the Day of Atonement rituals accomplished exactly what the day's name itself suggests: comprehensive atonement for sin, including those sins committed inadvertently by the High Priest, his family, and the people.

A number of key things become particularly important at this point. Firstly, the detailed instructions in Leviticus 16 required the High Priest to enter the Holy of Holies as part of his ministrations. As we have seen, this was the only occasion that anybody was allowed to do this, and great care needed to be taken to enter that most holy and sacred place properly. Thus, Leviticus 16: 12 makes it very clear that he "shall take a censer full of coals of fire from the altar before the LORD, and two handfuls of sweet incense beaten small, and he shall bring it inside the veil and put the incense on the fire before the LORD, that the cloud of the incense may cover the mercy seat that is over the testimony, so that he does not die." Later we read that the High Priest must sprinkle some of the slaughtered bull's blood on the cover of the Ark in the Holy of Holies, and later that he must do the same thing with the slaughtered goat's blood.

Related to this activity in the Holy of Holies, however, is something that is crucial to an understanding of John's description of the tomb of Jesus on that resurrection morning: however odd this link between his gospel and the Levitical instructions concerning the Day of Atonement may at first appear. Leviticus 16 makes very clear that on the Day of Atonement the High Priest "must put on the holy linen coat and shall have the linen undergarment on his body, and he shall tie the linen sash round his waist, and wear the linen turban; these are the holy garments" (Leviticus 16: 4). Indeed, a significant part of the instructions contained in Leviticus 16 is given over to what the High Priest should wear and when and makes clear that for key parts of the Day of Atonement rituals – specifically those to do with what had to be done inside the Holy of Holies – he must wear simple linen: both for his body and, separately, for his head. However – and this is again crucial for an understanding of John's telling of the resurrection story – the High Priest was required to *take off* this linen and leave it behind before he exited the Temple. Leviticus 16: 23 makes this very clear in its instruction that the High Priest is to "come into the Tent of Meeting and shall take off the linen garments that he put on when he went into the Holy Place *and shall leave them there.*" (Italics mine).

Putting all of this together throws very clear – and, perhaps, somewhat unexpected – light on John's description of the arrangement of the items inside Jesus' tomb on that remarkable resurrection morning. Firstly, as with the High Priest on the Day of Atonement, Jesus has clearly been dressed in linen: in Jesus' case these are, of course, his wrappings as prepared and wrapped around him by Joseph of Arimathea and Nicodemus and found apparently 'unwrapped' by their earliest discoverers. And – again as with the High Priest – John makes clear that there were separate wrappings for the body and the head. We recall that Leviticus 16 distinguishes carefully between the linen that had to be worn around the body of the High Priest and the "linen turban" that was to cover his head. We may usefully compare this with John's description of Jesus' grave clothes as consisting of the linen cloths 'and the face cloth, which had been on Jesus' head, not lying with the linen cloths but folded up in a place by itself' (John 20: 7). Important also is what the High Priest was to do with the linen garments when he had completed the Day of Atonement rituals. As will be recalled, he was to *leave them behind*. Thus, the Law as set out in Leviticus 16 commanded their deliberate removal with active intent by the High Priest himself before his commencement of the remainder of the Day of Atonement ritual which involved bathing, putting on his usual garments, and emerging to offer his burnt offering and the burnt offering for the people. Indeed, with this, the ritual was effectively complete.

Throughout, however, Leviticus 16 is very clear about how the High Priest must be dressed. Thus Leviticus 16: 32 functions as something of a reminder: "[The] priest who is anointed...shall make atonement, wearing the holy linen garments." But once this had been done, the Law was equally clear that these holy linen garments were to be left behind and, in a sense, 'entombed.' That this recalls to mind the apparently deliberate removal of the linen by Jesus as set out by John should by now be clear. And it should be equally clear by this point in this book that this 'chimes in' neatly – and, in a sense, predictably - with John's consistent portrayal throughout his gospel of Jesus as one who embodies in his person the Temple: with all that this means.

Thus, when the 'other disciple' is said by John to have seen *and* believed, it is surely more than even a man rising from the dead that is being suggested as regards *what* he believed. A priestly insider, viewing events with a 'priestly eye', sees the linen deliberately and carefully left behind and realises that this is the very thing that the High Priest was required to do on the Day of Atonement. Here is the turban! And here is the rest of the linen! Left behind! Just as the High Priest would leave them behind when atonement had been made and sins forgiven! Perhaps their removal had even been one of that disciple's priestly duties. Given everything that John has said about Jesus as the Temple up to this point in his gospel – and given the distinct allusion to Jesus as High Priest in his depiction of the events surrounding the crucifixion – it is surely no surprise that he presents Jesus in his death and resurrection as once again performing a crucial Temple function as its High Priest in leaving the holy linen behind on the Day of Atonement when all has been completed.

'As She Wept, She Stooped to Look'

But has all *really* been completed? Is this all that John has to say about the relationship of this tomb and its contents to the Temple? There is one other 'player' in this drama that we have yet to fully consider: Mary. And as we pick up John's story again and focus on Mary's role in it we realise that in his description of what was in the tomb on that momentous morning John is making no vague allusion that its details 'might be' viewed in terms reminiscent of the Temple and its contents: he is positively spelling it out for us.

It is not made clear by John why at the climactic moment of discovery and realisation of the vacated tomb Peter and the other disciple simply decide to go back to their homes. Indeed, given the momentousness of the discovery, this seems distinctly *anti*-climactic. But John now re-introduces another character into his narrative whose own discoveries will be anything but anti-climactic. We read that even as the two disciples are making their way back into the city Mary is weeping outside of the tomb. Perhaps with both men now departed she wants to make her own observations, and we read that as she wept 'she stooped to look into the tomb' (John 20: 11). And what she sees next is greater even than anything that the two men saw, for, as John tells it, 'she saw two angels in white, sitting where the body of Jesus had lain, one at the head and one at the feet' (John 20: 12). Given what we have already noted about the construction and layout of first-century Jewish burial tombs it is highly tempting to speculate that, stooping low, she is enabled to look directly into the tomb and up and directly at the niche where the body of Jesus had once lain. Perhaps the tomb faced east, as some early traditions have indicated, and the as-yet low sun's dim light gives just enough illumination to see. Or perhaps the previous events have taken up sufficient time for the sun to have fully risen. Either way, what Mary sees is remarkable: two angels, one at one end of the niche and one at the other, where Jesus' head and feet once were.

Whilst the ensuing and brief conversation between Mary and the angels might be of interest, of more interest for our current purposes is the actual *location* of the angels. John's description of them as being at the head and feet of where Jesus had lain might simply reflect a practical arrangement: after all, in a new rock-hewn tomb it might have been the only place they *could* sit. But, as ever in John's gospel, it is clear that something more is being suggested. As we have already noted, the original Tabernacle and later the first Temple contained within the Holy of Holies the Ark of the Covenant which had been so central to the experience of the Israelites in their journey to the Promised Land. We noted also that there was a very distinctive arrangement atop the Ark, with cherubim placed either side of it. And now we read in John that two angels – one at each end – occupied a very specific location within the tomb, being seated at either end of the niche where Jesus' lifeless body had once been.

What *could* John be telling us? In view of the fact that he has already gone to great lengths to connect the tomb with the Temple's holiest places in his description of the location of the left-behind linen, it seems likely that he is making the connection again by depicting the location of the angels. It is as if he is making clear in his description of the presence of the angels and their being situated at either end of something (or, at least, a now-departed something) that we are to view this tomb as if it was the Holy of Holies. Just as the original Temple's holiest place had contained a locus of the divine presence protected by angels, so too, it seems, does this tomb. So when Mary stoops to look into what is ostensibly an ordinary rock-hewn tomb it is as if she is stooping to look into the Holy of Holies. And – lo and behold! – she sees the angels, only in this instance they are living, speaking angels and there is no Ark for them to stand either side of: just an empty niche where Jesus' body had been. A stone bench where the divine presence had recently lain.

'A Hanged Man Is Cursed By God'

As we saw at the beginning of this chapter, for Jews nothing defiled like death. No tomb could be located to the West of the city in order to avoid anything corrupting any of its holiest places; the Temple foremost amongst them. Yet here is John, apparently showing that there is some kind of equivalence between the Temple's holiest place and a simple tomb in which the body of a crucified man had been lain. To say that this is unexpected is an understatement. It is a twist *par excellence*;

at once subversive and shocking, particularly given the horror and disgrace with which crucifixion was viewed in Jesus' day. Deuteronomy 22-23 makes clear that "if a man has committed a crime punishable by death and he is put to death, and you hang him on a tree, his body shall not remain all night on the tree, but you shall bury him the same day, for a hanged man is cursed by God. You shall not defile your land that the LORD your God is giving you as an inheritance." This was how crucifixion was viewed: as a death so dreadful that its victim was seen as cursed and his crucified body seen as a potent source of defilement to the extent that the whole land of Israel was at risk from its effects if it was permitted to stay unburied overnight. Such certainly explains the haste with which Jesus' burial was attended to by Joseph of Arimathea and Nicodemus.

But now, within the climax of his narrative, here is John telling us that Mary saw angels where the head and feet of this body had been. A place of utter defilement is a Holy Place; is, in fact, the Holiest of Places! It is a momentous reversal: and one which is deeply ironic. Indeed, such are the implications of this unexpected turn of events that we must return to them in the chapter that follows.

Chapter Nine: A Temple Torn Down

Strange Signs

There were those who watched the mayhem on the day that Jesus made his whip of cords and caused a commotion in the Temple who would see things that were even stranger and yet more puzzling. Unusual and unsettling things: both in the sky and on the ground. Josephus chronicles some of these in his book *The Jewish War*, describing events – ordinary, odd, and dreadful - that occurred in the decades immediately following Jesus' crucifixion. He tells us, for example, about a star that 'stood over the City, very like a broadsword' which, together with a comet, 'remained a whole year.' Whilst the exact year of this dual event is not specified, he tells us that afterwards, on a Passover and lasting half an hour, 'so bright a light shone around the Altar and the Sanctuary that it might have been midday.' The Temple was clearly the scene of other unusual events at this time as well and Josephus tells us that at the very same Passover 'a cow brought by someone to be sacrificed gave birth to a lamb in the middle of the Temple courts, while at midnight it was observed that the East Gate of the inner court had opened of its own accord'; a gate, which, he adds, was 'made of bronze and so solid that every evening twenty strong men were required to shut it.' This was clearly an event that caused some disquiet: 'The temple guards ran with the news to the Captain [of the Temple], who came up and by a great effort managed to shut it.' What could this possibly mean? Josephus says that opinion was divided. Whilst 'the laity' perceived it as '"he best of omens', there were others – 'the learned' - who discerned in this strange event 'that the Sanctuary was dissolving of its own accord, and that the opening of the gate was a gift of the enemy; and they admitted in their hearts that the sign was a portent of desolation.' (*Jewish War* 6.5.3 288-309).

Armies and Omens

As odd as this series of events might have been, much odder events were to follow. Josephus tells us that shortly after this Passover, five or six weeks later, an event occurred which was almost 'too amazing to be believed' and which would, he supposed, 'have been dismissed as an invention, had it not been vouched for by eyewitnesses and followed by disasters that bore out the signs.' On this occasion, the 21st of Artemisios by Josephus' reckoning: 'Before sunset there were seen in the sky, over the whole country, chariots and regiments in arms speeding through the clouds and encircling the towns.' But then, surpassing even this, at an (undated) Pentecost we learn that 'when the priests had gone into the inner court of the Temple at night to perform the usual ceremonies, they declared that they were aware, first of a violent movement and a loud crash, then of a concerted cry: "Let us go hence."'" (*Jewish War* 6.5.3 288-309).

A discerning observer of these events might have linked them with other odd and ominous occurrences that had been happening in and around the Temple for some time and which are recounted in the Talmud. It records, for example, that the centre lamp of the candelabrum which burned in the Holy Place mysteriously went out. Given that this lamp symbolized God's presence in the Temple it is tempting to link this event with the cry "Let us go hence" that Josephus records. Could it be that what was happening was a series of signs indicating that the Temple was in some sort of danger? Or that God's displeasure rested in some way upon it and that He had left or was about to leave it? Other events seemed to reinforce these suspicions, many centred around rituals that were intrinsically bound up with activities in the Temple. On the Day of Atonement, for example, the goat that was to be killed – as opposed to the scapegoat – was tied to the Temple door with a crimson thread. Whilst this thread had historically – and apparently miraculously – changed colour, it failed to do so for several decades in the middle of the first century. This was the source of some disquiet. The changing of colour from crimson to white was widely interpreted in the light of Isaiah 1:18: "Though your sins are like scarlet, they shall be white as snow; though they are red like crimson, they shall become like wool." But now that the thread was failing to change colour a question inevitably arose: were the Day of Atonement rituals now failing to secure atonement for the sins of the people? And if so, why? Something was clearly wrong, and this sense was reinforced by other oddities associated with the Day of Atonement rituals. The choosing of which goat would be the scapegoat and which one would be sacrificed – the one 'for the Lord', as it was known - had always been done by the drawing of a lot. Incredibly, for four decades near the beginning of the first century and thus at the same time that the other mysterious events were unfolding, the Lot for the Lord always came up in the High Priest's left hand: an incredibly statistically improbable event and one which was once again interpreted as revealing Divine displeasure (*Yoma* 39b). Omen upon omen; sign upon sign.

And, like Josephus, the Talmud too records the oddity of the strange and inexplicable nocturnal opening of the Temple doors. It recounts that when the doors mysteriously opened, Rabbi Yohannan ben Zakkai actually spoke to the Temple, saying: "O Temple, why do you frighten us? We know that you will end up destroyed. For it has been said, 'Open your doors, O Lebanon, that the fire may devour your cedars!'" (Zechariah 11:1) (*Sota* 6:3). Reflecting on many of the strange events both in the sky and on the ground that seemed to accumulate as the first century went on, Josephus muses that these unmistakable signs were disregarded by the majority of the people, 'as if they were moonstruck, blind and senseless.' But for those few with eyes to see and ears to hear, it was clear that deeper and more ominous signals were being sent.

An Approaching Storm

Seemingly hand-in-hand with these unusual omens, events both more mundane and more terrible were playing out in and around Israel and, finally, in Jerusalem itself. In 66 CE, just one year after Herod's magnificent Temple was finally finished, there was a major uprising against the Romans by many Jews and this was to set in motion a train of events which was to continue apace until a dreadful climax was reached. Cestius Gallus, Roman Governor of Syria, took the twelfth legion and set about putting down the Jewish rebellion. Having destroyed Zebulon in Galilee he turned south and surrounded Jerusalem, arriving during the Feast of Tabernacles. Incredibly he was defeated, and the following year Rome declared war on Israel: a conflict which could only have one outcome. The emperor Nero sent Vespasian with an army of 60,000 men and much bloodshed followed, first in Galilee. Meanwhile, in Jerusalem, there was factionalism and infighting among various Jewish groups with the city effectively being divided into three main factions comprised of Zealots, Galileans and Idumeans. In June 68 CE Vespasian reached Jerusalem and a siege began. Temporary respite for its inhabitants followed when Nero died and the 'Year of Four Emperors' ensued which culminated in Vespasian himself being made Emperor. In the end, in 69 CE, Emperor Vespasian sent his son, Titus, to Jerusalem to continue the assault.

A dreadful series of events now ensued. Weakened by hunger and internal factionalism the Jews defended the city heroically but at the end of a siege lasting five months the city walls were breached. Inevitable slaughter followed with the Romans fighting house to house to subdue the city. Finally, on the 9th of Av, on the very anniversary of the destruction of the first Temple, Herod's Temple was set ablaze. Its defenders fought with all of the zeal that would be expected, given that the Temple's destruction was now imminent. Some threw themselves onto the Roman swords. Some threw themselves into the flames. As the Temple stones burned their limestone content expanded and they actually exploded. In one day, the Temple was burned to the ground and completely destroyed. Josephus, an eyewitness to these dreadful events, writes that:

> 'While [the Temple] was on fire, everything was plundered that came to hand, and ten thousand of those that were caught were slain; nor was there a commiseration of any age…but children and old men…and priests, were all slain in the same manner…The flame was also carried a long way, and made an echo, together with the groans of those that were slain…one would have thought the whole city would have been on fire. Nor can one imagine anything greater and more terrible than this noise.' (*Jewish War* 6. 271 ff.)

As a result of these events the Temple – the very Temple that Jesus knew and walked in and in which generations of Jews had worshipped and sacrificed - was utterly and completely destroyed. Only the platform atop Mount Moriah upon which it had rested was left. An early tradition recorded and preserved in the Talmud had boasted that 'He who has not seen the Temple of Herod has never seen a beautiful building' (*Bava Basra* 4a). But after the events that had culminated in its destruction on the 9th of Av in 70 CE its beauty was consigned to living memory and subsequently to the pages of recorded history alone.

A National Calamity

It is almost impossible to overstate the magnitude of this calamity for the Jewish people: then, as now. As this book has already made clear, the Temple was far, far more than a place of daily sacrifice and annual pilgrimage. Israel had lost its national centre and with this its centre for worship, art and music too. It had lost the repository for its funds, the place at which its annual calendar was set, and a place that had inspired the awe of the nations. But more even than this, it had lost the very House of its God and the place of access to His most holy presence. And if tradition and belief are to be followed, the Universe had lost its very microcosm and centre and the place to which the Prophets had promised that one day all nations would make pilgrimage. It was a national and universal tragedy, but the blow would be felt by Israel alone. For their part, the Romans celebrated the event by minting coins proclaiming that Israel had been destroyed, whilst, back in Rome, the sack and looting of the Temple was commemorated by the building of an arch – the Arch of Titus - that still stands. It shows the carrying away into distant lands of Jewish slaves and booty alike.

The Jewish people were now faced with questions that went to the heart of their traditions and culture and by an event which threatened their very existence. How could the requirements of the Law be met in the absence of a Temple? How could forgiveness of sins be secured now that there was no Holy of Holies for the High Priest to go into on the annual Day of Atonement? How could the founding events of Israel's history be commemorated and remembered now that there was no place of pilgrimage for her scattered people? Could the nation with its distinctive culture and traditions survive this historical, spiritual and cultural calamity? How could it carry on now that the house of its God lay ruined and its people decimated, demoralized, and sold into slavery to the extent that the price of a Jewish slave was now less than the price of a horse? If the sight of the Temple in flames had been like the witnessing of the end of the world, what could possibly follow?

To have died without living through these events might have been considered a blessing and to have escaped the slaughter and plunder that occurred during and after the destruction of Jerusalem and its Temple might have been considered a deliverance: at least of sorts. And in these ways the early Jerusalem Christian community appears to have been quite fortunate. Early Christian history records that before the destruction of Jerusalem and as a result of apparently divine revelation the community had fled the city and moved temporarily to Pella in the region of the Decapolis before returning when the dreadful events had run their course. Epiphanius of Salamis, a late fourth century Bishop with access to earlier traditions, records that Jesus revealed to Jerusalem's Christians that they should leave and that afterwards the disciples of the disciples of the apostles flourished in the faith and worked great signs upon their return to the city after their temporary sojourn across the Jordan.

Great Lights Extinguished

But this community would be notable not for who belonged to it but for who no longer belonged to it. By the time of the destruction of Jerusalem and the events which followed this many of the early followers of Jesus were no more. Tradition records that Peter died by being crucified upside down in around 67 CE - at about the same time as Paul - at the time of Nero's persecution of the Early Church. James the brother of Jesus and an early leader of the Jerusalem church died in either 62 or 69 CE as a result of being pushed from the highest pinnacle of the Temple and then being clubbed to death after having incredibly survived the fall. Acts records that James, the son of Zebedee, had been put to death even earlier: at the time of Herod Agrippa in 44 CE. And as the century wore on history and tradition record that more apostles died or, like Bartholemew, simply disappeared from view.

But the church continued to grow as the traditions handed on by the earliest apostles were passed down to their successor disciples. Hierarchies and church offices developed as it became necessary to lead and administer these still-early Christian communities and the church continued to expand well beyond its roots in Israel. By the late second century there was a thriving church at Ephesus in Asia and it is from there that a fragment of a letter from one Polycrates, a bishop of the Ephesian church, has survived. Its subject-matter appears to have been a controversy that had developed within the early Christian churches and which was in full flow during his lifetime: the so-called 'Quartodeciman Controversy.' This centred on the issue of when Easter should be celebrated. The churches in Asia celebrated it on 14th Nisan as a sort of 'Christian Passover' and it thus fell annually on whatever day of the week 14th Nisan was in that particular year. By contrast, the church in Rome decreed that it should be celebrated on the Sunday following that date. The debate rumbled on and Polycrates' letter has been dated to the end of the second century and appears to have been directed to Bishop Victor of Rome.

It is interesting insofar as in addition to defending the Ephesian practice of celebrating Easter on 14th Nisan it also alludes to what Polycrates himself had seen and heard and what he had inherited from others concerning the deaths of early Christian apostles and notables. Thus, he writes: 'For indeed in Asia great luminaries have fallen asleep, such as shall rise again on the day of the Lord's appearing, when he comes with glory from heaven to seek out all his saints...' In this vein, he mentions 'Philip, one of the twelve apostles, who has fallen asleep in Hierapolis, [as have] also his two daughters who grew old, in virginity, and his other daughter who lives in the Holy Spirit and rests at Ephesus...' But then he writes something even more interesting, particularly in view of what this book has been uncovering. He mentions 'John also, he who leaned back on the Lord's breast' and we at once understand that it is the blessed disciple, the disciple whom Jesus loved, none other than John himself, whose death Polycrates is alluding to. And then he adds that this John 'was a priest, wearing the High Priestly frontlet, both witness and teacher. He has fallen asleep at Ephesus.'

This is a truly remarkable claim. For whilst the association of John with Ephesus in his later years is well-attested elsewhere and is generally accepted – being found in the writings of various Christian writers including the Church Father Irenaeus – the notion that he was a priest seems flatly contradicted by the generally accepted view that this John was none other than the brother of James, the son of Zebedee, and a fisherman before (and temporarily after) his calling by Jesus. How, then, can Polycrates describe him as a *priest*? In fact, Polycrates appears to go even further in his letter to Bishop Victor, stating that this John was in fact a *High Priest*. The reference to the fact that he wore the High Priestly frontlet – *to petalon* – is a clear one and is presumably intended to convey to Bishop Victor exactly what kind of priest he was. In short, and based on what he knows as a native of Ephesus, Polycrates appears to be claiming nothing other than the fact that this John, the disciple whom Jesus loved and the author of the gospel that bears his name, had been at one time during his life a serving High Priest.

John the High Priest

It is not the purpose of this book to discuss in detail the myriad and sometimes complex theories and points of view that have been put forward regarding the identity of the author of the Gospel of John. These would fill a book of their own. It will be enough simply to state that what we have learned up to this point would seem to lend some credence to Polycrates' claim – remarkable as that claim sounds. For, as we have seen, there is clear internal evidence within the Gospel of John that its author was indeed some kind of 'priestly insider': that he views events with a 'priestly eye' and has a concern to show Jesus as the reality that somehow 'stands behind' and fulfils the functions of the earthly Temple, including its priestly and High Priestly functions. That this concern might have been uppermost in the mind of an ex-priest or High Priest seems likely and would explain the distinctive perspective on events that John's gospel takes when viewed against those of Matthew, Mark and Luke. Perhaps, given the recent concern to understand the origins of Christianity in the light of the events surrounding the Temple and its destruction – a concern which this book in large part shares – it is time to re-examine the evidence for the authorship of John's gospel and to re-evaluate the claim that Polycrates makes in his letter. That will be for others to undertake, should they choose.

For now, and as this book reaches its conclusion, it is tempting to see in the twin facts of the destruction of the Temple and the identity of John as a priestly insider – perhaps even a High Priest – some further pieces of a jigsaw which we have been assembling from the beginning. During his younger years John had spent some considerable time with his Lord, sitting at his feet hearing sometimes incomprehensible things and witnessing events that carried meanings that could only be understood in hindsight. Perhaps he was there in the Temple courts on the day that his Lord turned over the tables, scattered the animals, and claimed to be a Temple that would rise again even if it was to be destroyed. He was certainly there and leaning on his Lord's breast on the night of the betrayal, an event that would gain him the sort of nickname that Polycrates reproduces in his letter to Bishop Victor: 'he who leaned back on the Lord's breast.' He was at the foot of the cross as well: standing so close that he could see the blood and water flowing from his Lord's pierced side. And he was there with Peter on that incredible morning when, responding to Mary's breathless claims of an empty tomb, they discovered the strips of linen deliberately discarded: the final piece of a puzzle which John had no doubt pondered over many times and which finally made sense of the whole. Thus, John's gospel tells us: he saw *and believed*.

And throughout it all he saw things as a priest would, discerning the meaning and significance of his Lord's words and actions in the light of the remarkable claim that this man was, somehow, *the* Temple: the *real* one, and standing in relation to the earthly one as an original would stand in relation to a copy or a light would stand in relation to a shadow. And in the final years of his life, at Ephesus, he once again pondered the meaning of these things in the light of events which many of the disciples and apostles did not live to see. For John - living to remarkable old age if many early traditions are to be believed - would certainly have known that the Jerusalem Temple had been destroyed, and would have been in possession of this knowledge when he wrote his gospel. Whilst he may not have heard the dreadful sounds and seen the dreadful sights that accompanied its destruction he would have felt the blow as keenly as any Jew: more so, if he had once served within it as a priest or someone even greater. And as any Jew would, John would have surely pondered over the meaning of this dreadful event but with a perspective informed by his knowledge of what his Lord had said and done. The Temple was destroyed but this man had claimed to be a Temple that could *never* be destroyed. Indeed, they *had* sought to destroy him, but death could not hold him, and in the light of this John would realise many things: not least that what this man had claimed to be gave hope even in the midst of the darkness of the earthly Temple's complete and total destruction. *A* Temple had been destroyed but *the* Temple had not and could not be destroyed. And so John wrote his gospel: to demonstrate the proof and meaning of this and to share with his readers the remarkable implications that followed so that they, too, might see and believe.

Chapter Ten: "If You Forgive The Sins Of Any, They Are Forgiven…"

On the evening of that day, the first day of the week, the doors being locked for fear of the Jews, Jesus came and stood among them and said to them, "Peace be with you." When he had said this, he showed them his hands and his side. Then the disciples were glad when they saw the Lord. Jesus said to them again, "Peace be with you. As the Father has sent me, even so I am sending you." And when he had said this, he breathed on them and said to them, "Receive the Holy Spirit. If you forgive the sins of any, they are forgiven them; if you withhold forgiveness from any, it is withheld."

John 20: 19- 23

Corkscrews and Consciousness

Inspiration can come from the most unlikely sources and on the most unexpected of occasions and I discovered this time and time again both whilst researching *Temple and Tomb* and during the writing process itself. One such occasion sticks in my mind because what I had been thinking about leading up to it was far removed from John's gospel. For some years I have taught Philosophy alongside Religious Studies and one topic – the Philosophy of Mind – has frequently engendered lively discussion amongst my students. This area of Philosophy explores the nature of mind and consciousness, how they might be explained philosophically, and what relationship they might have – if any – to the brain. The question of whether or not *computers* might have minds is one which my students find particularly interesting. One philosophical theory known as functionalism argues that maybe computers *do* have minds if you are prepared to view a mind as a set of arrangements in which input – for example sensory input - is converted

143

into output in the form of states of mind, behaviour, or other action. So, this theory goes, if a mind is seen in this way we should be prepared to ascribe minds – and by extension, consciousness – to computers, given that they 'specialize' in turning input (the movement of my fingers on the keyboard as I type this, for example) into output (such as words on a screen and, by extension, words on a page).

This theory inevitably leads to the question: just exactly *what* is it that turns the input into output? In the case of a human mind the answer is frequently given that it is the brain, but some functionalists argue that this doesn't really matter. Anything will do, they argue, as long as the function is performed. In technical language, they say that the set of arrangements is 'multiply realisable'. In other words, various ways of performing the function are possible, as long as the function is performed.

Many standard Philosophy textbooks use the example of a corkscrew to illustrate how a set of arrangements might be multiply realisable. A corkscrew's function is in essence to take input in the form of a bottle with a cork and to convert it into output in the form of an opened bottle, but there are various ways in which corkscrews do this. Some you just insert into the cork and tug. Some have 'wings' that come up on either side as the corkscrew is twisted into the cork and which you press down on to lever the cork out. Some you fix to the kitchen work surface and insert the neck of the bottle into. Some even force compressed air into the bottle which drives the cork upwards and outwards with a 'pop'. Thus, the set of arrangements is said to be *multiply realisable*. As long as the bottle is opened, it doesn't much matter which way you do it. Various different sets of arrangements can produce the same result.

Unexpected Inspiration

In the midst of a discussion that was sparked by these thoughts and ideas I realised that I was thinking – quite unexpectedly – about John's gospel and Jesus' claim to be the Temple that we encounter there. It is sometimes difficult to separate what a thing is from what it does – or even what a person is or appears to be and what he or she does - and this difficulty seems in large part to underlie the confusion that Jesus' claim to be the Temple created in the minds of some of his hearers on that fateful occasion during Passover when he turned over the tables and drove the cattle out. "Destroy this temple, and in three days I will raise it up" Jesus shouts, meaning the Temple of his body. The reaction to this is mockery bordering on incredulity as 'The Jews' respond by saying: "It has taken forty-six years to build this temple, and will you raise it in three days?" John the 'intrusive narrator' then 'buts in' to the description of the event to make clear that Jesus was not talking about a building but his body, and that this truth only dawned on his disciples after he was raised from the dead. But in what sense was his body the Temple? Surely not in any kind of *literal* sense as some of his hearers on that occasion appear to have thought. We have already examined in detail the immensity and the grandeur of the Temple and its precincts that sat atop Mount Moriah during Jesus' lifetime. Jesus could hardly have been claiming to be *that*. But what if he was thinking in terms of what the Temple *did*? It's *function*, in other words?

Flesh and Stones

By the time we arrive at the end of his gospel it is clear that John has already prepared us to see Jesus and the Temple in terms of their shared functions. In fact, as we have seen, he has done so from the very beginning. He has shown us, for example, that like the Temple and the Tabernacle before it, Jesus is God's abiding presence in the midst of his people. So what Jesus *does* God *does*: from revealing his Father's will to doing his Father's works. In fact, John shows us time and again throughout his gospel that Jesus is the whole set of arrangements that the earthly Temple provides and as the narrative unfolds he gradually and systematically reveals him to be the one who joins Heaven and Earth, the forgiving presence, the source of living waters, the One who gives life to those that stay joined to him, the Passover sacrifice, the High Priest, and so on. In each case, John is telling us, what the Temple *does*, Jesus *does*. It is nothing to do with the size of the stones or the amount of time it has taken to put them together. Instead, it is all about shared *function*, with the real difference being that the earthly Temple is a shadow of Jesus and thus in some sense a copy of or substitute for him. So, for example, in equating Jesus with the Tabernacle in the Prologue he has pointed to Jesus as God's abiding presence with His people and as the source of his *revealing* presence. Just as God revealed His will from within the Tabernacle, says John, so too does He do this in and through Jesus. There is thus a function shared by the Tabernacle on the one hand and Jesus on the other that allows us to equate the two in terms of what they both *do*. Much the same sort of idea runs through the story of Jesus' encounter with the Samaritan woman. Just as the Temple functions as the source of living water in Ezekiel, so, too, does Jesus function as the source of living water, and John carries this idea over to his description and interpretation of the events on the last and greatest day of the Feast of Tabernacles as well. And this *motif* continues right up to the end of the gospel in John's portrayal of Jesus as the one in whom the festivals of Passover and Atonement find their ultimate meaning and reality. What they do, John says, Jesus does: but in the fullest and realest sense, and thus in an even *fuller* or *realer* sense. If he had the vocabulary, John might have said that the set of arrangements which the Temple provided was multiply realisable and as Messiah, Jesus will even *rebuild* the Temple and *has* done so: the real Temple of his body. Of course, John is a far more creative and subtle writer than this, and he expresses it all in a series of events and encounters vividly depicted and shot through with symbolism and subtleties of layered expression, as we have seen. But express it he does: consistently and throughout.

Given that when he wrote his gospel the Temple atop Mount Moriah was no more, the importance of a continuing, living, Temple that could never be destroyed would have attained the very highest importance. Little wonder that looking back on events John wrote such a 'Temple-centric' gospel. How could the world possibly survive a catastrophe such as the one which befell the Temple? The answer was to be found in Jesus, the *real* Temple that lives on even though the old one is no more: a Temple that is indestructible and thus continues to perform all of the functions that the old Temple once performed, but in their 'highest' and truest sense. And the irony of this, John tells us, is that the people to whom Jesus was sent either would not or could not see this: either during his lifetime or afterwards. The reader, however, is in a much better position to see it. Unlike many of the characters in the gospel the reader has not physically seen the events as they play out in 'real time' but he or she can still believe and this, says John, is why he wrote his gospel. As an insider, he knows full well the meaning of events that would be lost if the reader did not have such an insightful narrator and guide as he: one that can reveal what events *really* mean when viewed from the inside. Indeed, most of the characters who actually witnessed the events as they actually unfolded failed to understand them. But thanks to John, the reader can both see and believe and is invited to do so. The question then becomes: what difference should such belief make? Having seen and believed, what should the believer *do*?

The First Day

Given the remarkable events that occurred on the morning when Jesus was discovered to have risen from the dead it is perhaps easy to overlook the fact that remarkable events occurred during the evening of that day as well. But John, typically, is very clear about both the time that they occurred and the detail of those events. Almost at the very end of his gospel he tells us that 'On the evening of that day, the first day of the week, the doors being locked for fear of the Jews, Jesus came and stood among them and said to them, "Peace be with you." When he had said this, he showed them his hands and his side. Then the disciples were glad when they saw the Lord' (John 20: 19- 23). Thus far it has been Mary Magdalene alone who has seen him. Now the disciples (minus Thomas) have been privileged to see him too. But what is the purpose of the visit? John tells us that they were all together in a locked room, afraid. Perhaps the visit is to still their fears. Perhaps it is to provide physical proof of what they have so far only learned from a handful of testimonies alone. Or perhaps the visit is to bestow his peace, and hence the greeting. But what follows provides the real key to the meaning of this encounter, for immediately after the greeting and the description of the disciples' gladness we learn that 'Jesus said to them again, "Peace be with you. As the Father has sent me, even so I am sending you." And when he had said this, he breathed on them and said to them, "Receive the Holy Spirit. If you forgive the sins of any,

147

they are forgiven them; if you withhold forgiveness from any, it is withheld'" (John 20: 21-3).

This has traditionally been seen as a difficult passage and yet within it there is a clear message for the believer. Jesus has previously promised the Spirit and now he *gives* it, and with it a commission. Just as the Father sent him now he sends the disciples. But he does not send them alone to fend for themselves using their own strength and power. He gives them the Spirit that he has promised to give, and with it the authority – derived not from themselves but from he who gave it – to forgive or withhold forgiveness of sins. This is the most solemn giving and withholding there could possibly be but it is now possible because there stands before them the one who in his own body *is* the Temple: with all that this includes. What stones and priests and incense and festivals and sanctuaries and animal sacrifice provided the means for, Jesus has in his living, dying and risen body provided the *real* means for. And he delegates his authority over sin and death to the disciples and to all who believe because of them. Sins are forgiven, light has defeated darkness, and life has triumphed over death because of what Jesus the everlasting Temple has done. Now *go*, he says. Declare the forgiveness that I alone can give, for I am alive forevermore: a living Temple that can never be torn down.

Epilogue

The Jerusalem Temple together with what it once contained has provided a fertile source of inspiration for novelists and film-makers alike in recent decades. Perhaps the most well-known film portrayal of an important part of the Temple's content – and the quest to find it – is the 1981 blockbuster *Raiders of the Lost Ark*, featuring Harrison Ford as Indiana Jones. There can be few people who have not enjoyed this film and its dramatic portrayal of the hero's quest to find the Ark of the Covenant before a group of Nazis can harness its power to make their armies invincible. What is perhaps less well-known than this film is the fact that there have in recent years been a large number of real-life quests to find the Ark: all of these for various and sometimes quite diverse reasons.

In one recent and highly-readable attempt to track down the elusive Ark its author relates an episode within his particular quest in which he was discussing its whereabouts with a group of rabbis in Jerusalem. Of particular interest is their reaction to his search and recalling the event the author recounts the following exchange:

> "'It might sound naive to have a box as the vehicle of our God," a young American rabbi had said one earnest Shabbat-night dinner in Jerusalem. "But it's better than using our box as the vehicle for your theology." His thinly-bearded disciples put down their glasses and clapped, and looked to me for a response. What he meant was that the Ark has been hijacked by non-Jewish religions as a way of asserting that Judaism is hopelessly out of date.'

As brief as this exchange appears, when I read the words I was surprised at my own response to them and in particular at the disquiet I suddenly felt about researching and writing *Temple and Tomb*. Wasn't this exactly what *I* was trying to do? Wasn't this the place to which my own quest to understand John's gospel had led me? Wasn't I almost by implication asserting the very thing that the young rabbi was accusing

149

that author of asserting, except that I was asserting it of the whole Temple rather than just part of its content? I was troubled. And so, before this book closes, I would like to very briefly clarify what I have tried to do and what I have not tried to do and where I feel that *Temple and Tomb* has *really* led.

Firstly, in no way do I feel that I have 'hijacked' the Ark, and, by extension, the Temple that once housed it, as a 'vehicle' for some kind of different or 'superior' theology to the Judaism of which they were once such a central part. This was not my motivation in writing *Temple and Tomb*, nor do I believe that this is where its conclusions lead. In fact, I deeply admire the various different types of Judaism that exist in the world today and when I see how they flourish I see flowing streams of life-giving traditions that are very much up to date. It has seemed to me while writing this book that many events that occurred around the time that Herod's Temple was destroyed – including the destruction of the Temple itself – were the cause of that one flowing stream branching off into two. Indeed, history shows that Judaism survived the catastrophe that the destruction of its Temple created and that it became increasingly focussed on the Law and the Synagogue. In this way it survives and thrives still: to the betterment of humankind.

When Judaism 'forked' and became two streams, one of those went its own way and carved its own path and that became Christianity. And whilst it is unquestionably the case that Christianity and Judaism are now two very different traditions – or sets of traditions – it is clear to anybody who studies the history of the former that it is deeply indebted to the latter and simply would not exist without it: as this book has hopefully made clear. Far from being a box as a vehicle for some alien theology, the Ark – and the Tabernacle/Temple that originally existed to house it – is a reminder that without Judaism there could be no Jesus and no Christianity. I would rather see in Judaism and Christianity two very different yet related traditions, vigorous in health, flowing side by side. It is my hope that they will continue to flow their own courses – and maybe one day converge, when, as God says in Isaiah 11:9: "They shall not hurt or destroy in all my holy mountain, for the Earth shall be full of the knowledge of the Lord as the waters cover the sea."

Notes and References

Coming to the subject-matter – and particularly to the focus - of this book for the first time, a casual reader might assume that the understanding of Jesus' world as a 'Temple-centric' one was commonly held by Bible scholars: both historically and currently. That this is not, in fact, the case, makes the current book unusual, and at the time of writing it remains one of a very small number of studies to have attempted to view Jesus' teachings and actions in the specific light – or, perhaps it should be said, the specific shadow – of the Temple.

It is a rather different matter when *Temple and Tomb*'s context is broadened to include the Judaism – or, rather, Judaisms – of Jesus' day. Since the late 1970s – with some notable exceptions - it has become increasingly commonly assumed that the way to understand the Jesus of the gospels is one which assumes a continuity with – rather than a contrast to – the first century Judaisms that would have dominated the world of his thinking and being, and this includes the Gospel of John. The reader interested in this might be directed, for example, to E.P Sanders's *Jesus and Judaism*, (London, SCM, 1985); not least because the importance for Jesus' self-understanding of his demonstration in the Temple is dealt with at length here, although it will be clear that I do not follow Sanders in every respect and the focus of his book is certainly not on the Gospel of John. For a relatively recent – and less 'scholarly' – exploration of the continuity of Jesus' teaching with the thinking and teaching of many first-century rabbis, an excellent place to start would be Ann Spangler and Lois Tverberg's *Sitting at the Feet of Rabbi Jesus* (Michigan, Zondervan, 2009). In what follows I present the key texts – in addition to those cited, above - that have informed my own thinking and reflection on the relationship between Jesus and the Temple, with comments as appropriate.

No attempt to understand the importance of the Temple for first-century Jews can proceed without due acknowledgement of the contributions of archaeology to our understanding of both how that

Temple functioned and how important it was to those both inside and outside of Judea. In this respect, I drew much insight for the Introduction to *Temple and Tomb* from James Charlesworth (ed.), *Jesus and Temple: Textual and Archaeological Explorations* (Minneapolis, Fortress, 2014). Within that volume, Leen Ritmeyer's 'Imagining the Temple Known to Jesus and to Early Jews', Dan Bahat's 'The Second Temple in Jerusalem' and James H. Charlesworth's 'The Temple and Jesus' Followers' were particularly useful, as was Mordechai Aviam's extremely interesting paper 'Reverence for Jerusalem and the Temple in Galilean Society', from which I learned that reverence for the Temple would have extended far beyond Jerusalem and right the way to the Galilee of Jesus and the disciples. In addition, the whole study proved invaluable to my attempt in Chapter Three of this book to reconstruct what the apostolic band would have encountered as they actually progressed from outside the Temple to as far as they were allowed to go within it, as did the fourth chapter – 'Confronting the Establishment: Ruling Priests and the Temple'- of Craig A. Evans's immensely readable *Jesus and His World* (London, SPCK, 2012).

In reconstructing the history of the Tabernacle in Chapter Two of *Temple and Tomb* I obviously drew heavily on the relevant Old Testament sources as cited in the text, and the whole of the book draws on the English Standard Version unless otherwise stated. A study that was very informative as regards the construction of the Tabernacle and its relatedness to and continuity with the Temple at Jerusalem was T. Desmond Alexander and Simon Gathercole (eds), *Heaven on Earth: The Temple in Biblical Theology* (Carlisle, Paternoster, 2004). Here, the contributions from James Palmer ('Exodus and the Biblical Theology of the Tabernacle') and Pekka Pitkanen ('From Tent of Meeting to Temple: Presence, Rejection and Renewal of Divine Favour') were particularly useful. I was also indebted to F.F Bruce's masterful commentary on John and the Johannine epistles for my understanding of the Hebrew terms for aspects of the Tabernacle's construction and the significance of these for its relationship to Jesus (F.F Bruce, *The Gospel and Epistles of John*, Michigan, Eerdman's 1994).

One of the foremost sources of inspiration for any literary endeavour must be the author's own experiences, and my visit to the Kos asclepeion in 2010 provided much food for thought, particularly as I researched Jacob's dream of a ladder connecting heaven and earth. It was whilst at the Kos asclepeion that I learned of some of the odd experiences recounted in recent and not-so-recent times by pilgrims, visitors and temporary residents alike, and whilst my own dreams remained - comparatively - undisturbed by my visit I was moved both by the size of the complex and by the obvious sacrifices that many had made to get there in times past. As regards Jacob's dream, Seymour Rossel's *Bible Dreams: The Spiritual Quest* (Texas, Rossel Books, 2011) was invaluable as a source for understanding how rabbinic interpretation of this seminal event – past and present – has informed its understanding. The online *Jewish Virtual Library* was also a key resource throughout the researching of *Temple and Tomb*, not least it's extremely interesting and informative discussion of whether or not the site of Jacob's ladder was the same as that of the eventual Temple on Mount Moriah.

The relationship of Jesus to the Temple authorities has been foremost within many attempts to explain many of his attitudes towards it and actions within it. What was there about how the Temple was run – and by whom – that provoked his ire on that memorable day when he claimed so openly to *be* it? Originally, I wanted to call *Temple and Tomb* by the title 'Jesus the Temple' – given that this name summed up so much of what I wanted to say - but when I sat down to properly research it I found that Nicholas Perrin had already beaten me to it in his book of that name (London, SPCK, 2010). In fact, his whole study was invaluable as regards the ways in which many within the priesthood – including the High Priestly family – were viewed at the time of Jesus and it did much to throw light on why Jesus was so enraged by what he saw in the Temple courts. Mention should go too in this context to Chabad.org whose generous facility to 'ask the rabbi' allowed me to get a contemporary rabbinical perspective that confirmed much of what Perrin asserted.

As regards *Temple and Tomb*'s discussion of Jesus' encounter with the Woman of Samaria, his words and actions at the Festivals of Tabernacles and Dedication, and the significance of Jesus as High Priest, mention must be made of Mary Coloe's seminal study *God Dwells with Us: Temple Symbolism in the Fourth Gospel* (Minnesota,

Liturgical Press, 2001). Coloe's is the only study I know of that shares the specific aim of *Temple of Tomb*: to explore and to present the centrality of the Temple for John's understanding of who Jesus was and what Jesus did. It does this for a more academically-informed audience than *Temple and Tomb*, it draws some different conclusions, and it misses some of the climactic points that John is eager to make within his account of the resurrection and which I discuss in Chapters Eight and Ten, but it nonetheless belongs with the current study in its focussed concern to understand John's Jesus in the light of the Temple. Coloe's examination of Jesus' encounter with the Samaritan woman and her presentation of the significance of John's portrayal of events at the Festivals of Tabernacles and Dedication were of particular help as I researched these areas for Chapters Four and Five of this book and I refer the interested reader without hesitation to Coloe's ground breaking work. Whilst I do not intend *Temple and Tomb* to be in any sense a 'popularisation' of *God Dwells with Us*, I nonetheless concede that it would have been a very different book without Coloe's pioneering research. Only at the end of her examination of the gospel does she miss some of John's key points in relation to the functions performed both by Jesus and the Temple – and specifically those actions and functions performed historically by the High Priest - and I thus offer *Temple and Tomb*, in part, as a supplement – even, perhaps, as an extension - to her work for the interested (and perhaps less academically-trained) non-specialist.

John M. Lundquist's *The Temple* (London, Thames and Hudson, 1993) was also a key point of reference throughout the current study and particularly in Chapter Five. The notion of Temple-as-Omphalos was a particularly useful insight from this work, and did much to illuminate Jesus' invitation at the Festival of Tabernacles to come to him and drink. C.H Dodd's seminal commentary on John was also extremely useful as I sought to unpick the complexities of this notoriously difficult passage.

On the subject of difficult passages, Mary Coloe's insightful paper *Welcome into the Household of God: The Foot Washing in John 13* (The Catholic Biblical Quarterly, Volume 66, 2004) was a valuable source of information regarding what the foot washing in John 13 might both signify and *not* signify. The online *Jewish Encyclopaedia* proved an invaluable resource for my attempt to reconstruct the detail of the golden vine frieze above the entrance to the *naos* in Chapter Six of *Temple and Tomb*, as did Josephus' *The Jewish War* (5.5.4). I was also indebted throughout the study to Rabbi Norman Solomon's selected, translated and edited *The Talmud: A Selection* (London, Penguin, 2009), particularly for my attempt to reconstruct the Temple's layout and its operations.

My colleague Thom Russell at King Edward VI College, Stourbridge, gave invaluable advice regarding some of the subtleties of Greek grammar with which I needed to grapple, and he gave me some key insights into the complexities surrounding the use of conditional protasis with which I deal in Chapter Three. I was particularly indebted to Philip Harner's *The "I Am" of the Fourth Gospel* (London, Fortress, 1970) and F. Blass and A Debrunner's *A Greek Grammar of the New Testament and Other Early Church Literature* (Chicago, University of Chicago Press, 1961) as regards the unusual construction of the predicate noun accompanied by the definite article which I allude to in Chapter Six,

As the challenge of identifying John and assessing the possibility of how far he was an eye-witness to the events he describes became more important within *Temple and Tomb* – particularly in Chapter Seven - so too did the importance of Richard Bauckham's celebrated *Jesus and the Eyewitnesses: The Gospels as Eyewitness Testimony* (Michigan, Eerdman's, 2006). His masterly summary and examination of the roles of Papias, Polycrates and Irenaeus in the identification of the Beloved Disciple were particularly invaluable to the research and writing of Chapters Seven and Nine.

One of the joys of researching the current study came from casting my net as wide as possible and finding that, as a result, some key insights came from sources that I would not, as a rule, go to. In this respect, for example, due mention must be made of William J. Hamblin's *"I Have Revealed Your Name": The Hidden Temple in John 17* (Interpreter, Volume 1, Issue 1, pp. 61-89). Whilst standing outside of what might be considered to be 'mainstream' New Testament – and specifically Johannine – scholarship, Hamblin's skilful reconstruction of the historical and theological context of John's discourse to the disciples in

John 17 did much to help my quest to understand Jesus as High Priest in the fullest possible sense and as a result contributed much to Chapters Seven and Eight. I was indebted to Coloe, again, for the source of Chapter Seven's assertion that the blood and water flowing from Jesus' side matched what typically happened in and around the Temple altar at Passover time, and for the medical significance of this I would direct the interested reader to Pierre Barbet's *A Doctor at Calvary: The Passion of Our Lord Jesus Christ as Described by a Surgeon* (Allegro Reprints, 2014). For an overview of this and other contributors to the growing – but unusual – world of 'crucifixion science', I refer the interested reader to Max Hartshorn's extremely illuminating article *The Strange World of Crucifixion Science* (Fortean Times, April 2015, pp. 38-41).

When I first conceived of some of the ideas that *Temple and Tomb* explores in its closing chapters they were as parts of a very different book to the one that eventually emerged. In fact, my initial inspiration for the whole book came from a reference in Mark Stibbe's book *The Resurrection Code: Mary Magdalene and the Easter Enigma* (Milton Keynes, Authentic Media, 2008). It was here that I first realised the significance of the strips of linen for an understanding of John's resurrection narrative – and for John's identification of Jesus as High Priest - and my initial intention was to focus on the tomb's layout, contents, and constituent parts as a kind of 'counterpart' to the Temple with its dual division of the *naos* into the Holy Place and the Holy of Holies and its 'Ark' 'guarded' by cherubs at each end: the very thing that Mary Magdalene sees as she stoops to look into the emptied tomb. From here I was going to expand on this within the context of John's masterful use of irony overall and I fully intended to end with the observation that John's gospel attempts to show that the Temple was a 'type' or forerunner of Jesus' tomb. Irony of ironies! The Holiest Place was really a place of corruption and death all along; with the defilement usually associated with a tomb being itself transformed into a place of life and hope and glory! While I still think that some sort of study could be written along these lines, *Temple and Tomb* ultimately took a different direction and ended with a rather fuller scope. Because his focus was in large part on Mary Magdalene's role in the Easter story, Stibbe did not attempt to link his observations regarding the meaning of the death and resurrection narratives in John's gospel to that author's consistent assertion of Jesus *as* Temple, and in the end this fuller picture was too attractive (and too obvious) to miss. But I am indebted to Stibbe for both the initial inspiration for *Temple and Tomb* and for some of its later claims about Jesus as the High Priest making final atonement and leaving his High Priestly strips of linen behind; entombed for Peter and John to discover, as I discuss in Chapter Eight of this book.

As regards the actual details of the burial of Jesus which are also discussed in Chapter Eight, James H. Charlesworth's edited collection of essays *The Tomb of Jesus and His Family? Exploring Ancient Jewish Tombs Near Jerusalem's Walls* (Michigan, Eerdman's 2013) was a particularly invaluable resource, as were the references to burial customs in John J. Rousseau and Rami Arav's *Jesus and His World* (London, SCM, 1995). As regards the differences between the Shroud of Turin and the actual burial cloths that Jesus, as a first-century Jew, would have been likely to have been buried in, Ian Wilson's *The Shroud: Fresh Light on the 2000-Year-Old Mystery* (London, Transworld, 2010) contains all of the illustrations needed for the interested reader to make up his or her own mind.

Chapter Nine of this study, containing, as it does, frequent reference to the destruction of Herod's Temple and the dreadful events that accompanied this, was particularly harrowing to write. Josephus' *The Jewish War* was the obvious source, and the implications of the destruction of the Temple for the earliest Christians became more and more apparent as my research for that chapter unfolded. Bauckham's discussion of Polycrates' letter to Bishop Victor was of direct relevance as I sought to develop and explore my strong suspicion of John as 'Priestly Insider', but I would not attempt to defend too vigorously what remains but a tantalising possibility: that the author of the Gospel of John *might*, at some point, have served in the Jerusalem Temple as High Priest.

In addition to Mark Stibbe's impressive attempt to show the significance of the strips of linen for John's identification of Jesus as atoning High Priest, one other moment of inspiration provided the impetus to get *Temple and Tomb* started. It was, as I have described in the book's tenth chapter, in the actual midst of a philosophical discussion of Functionalism as a philosophical 'model' of mind with my college students. As regards the possibility of any set of arrangements – the Temple's included – being multiply realisable, many examples might be produced to illustrate the point. The corkscrew example that I use in *Temple and Tomb* is the same one I use with my students in our philosophical discussions, and I borrowed it from Sue Johnson et al, *Understanding Philosophy* (London, Nelson Thornes, 2005).

The writing of any book can be quite accurately described as a journey and, like any journey, being joined by agreeable companions on the way can brighten even the dullest moments. In this regard, special mention must be made of Charles Foster's *Tracking the Ark of the Covenant* (Oxford, Monarch, 2007). Part history book, part travelogue, part detective story, it details the author's own attempt to trace the Ark's history, with a view to finding where – if anywhere – it might have ended up. Perhaps unsurprisingly, Foster fails to find any contemporary trace of one of history's most sacred relics, but his book is a delight from start to finish. I was particularly struck by his encounter with the group of Jerusalem rabbis that I allude to in *Temple and Tomb*'s Epilogue, with its timely reminder of the perils and traps that await anybody's attempt to make what belongs to someone else their own.

Bibliography

Alexander, T. and Gathercole, S. (eds) (2004) *Heaven on Earth: The Temple in Biblical Theology*, Carlisle, Paternoster.

Barbet, P, (2014) *A Doctor at Calvary: The Passion of Our Lord Jesus Christ as Described by a Surgeon*, Allegro reprints.

Bauckham, R. (2006) *Jesus and the Eyewitnesses: The Gospels as Eyewitness Testimony*, Michigan, Eerdmans.

Blass, F. and Debrunner, A. (1961) *A Greek Grammar of the New Testament and Other Early Church Literature*, Chicago, University of Chicago Press.

Bruce, F. (1994) *The Gospel and Epistles of John*, Michigan, Eerdmans.

Charlesworth, J (ed) (2013) *The Tomb of Jesus and His Family? Exploring Ancient Jewish Tombs Near Jerusalem's Walls*, Michigan, Eerdmans.

Charlesworth, J (ed) (2014) *Jesus and Temple: Textual and Archaeological Explorations*, Minneapolis, Fortress.

Coloe, M. (2001) *God Dwells with Us: Temple Symbolism in the Fourth Gospel*, Minnesota, Liturgical Press.

Coloe, M. (2004) *Welcome into the Household of God: The Foot Washing in John 13*, The Catholic Biblical Quarterly, Volume 66.

Culpepper, R. (1983) *Anatomy of the Fourth Gospel: A Study in Literary Design*, Philadelphia, Fortress Press.

Dodd, C.H. (2008) *The Interpretation of the Fourth Gospel*, Cambridge, Cambridge University Press.

Evans, C. (2012) *Jesus and His World*, London, SPCK.

Foster, C. (2007) *Tracking the Ark of the Covenant*, Oxford, Monarch.

Hamblin, W. (2014) *"I Have Revealed Your Name": The Hidden Temple in John 17*, Interpreter, Volume 1, Issue 1.

Harner, P. (1970) *The "I Am" of the Fourth Gospel*, London, Fortress.

Hartshorn, M. (2015) *The Strange World of Crucifixion Science*, Fortean Times issue 327.

Lundquist, J. (1993) *The Temple*, London, Thames and Hudson.

Johnson, S. et al (2005) *Understanding Philosophy*, London, Nelson Thornes.

Josephus, F. (1981 edn) *The Jewish War,* London, Penguin.

Perrin, N. (2010) *Jesus the Temple*, London, SPCK.

Rossel, S. (2011) *Bible Dreams: The Spiritual Quest*, Texas, Rossel Books.

Rousseau, J. and Arav, R. (1995) *Jesus and His World*, London, SCM.

Sanders, E. (1985) *Jesus and Judaism*, London, SCM.

Solomon, N (ed) (2009) *The Talmud*, London, Penguin.

Spangler, A. and Tverberg, L. (2009) *Sitting at the Feet of Rabbi Jesus*, Michigan, Zondervan.

Stibbe, M. (1994) *John as Storyteller: Narrative, Criticism and the Fourth Gospel*, Cambridge, Cambridge University Press.

Stibbe, M. (2008) *The Resurrection Code: Mary Magdalene and the Easter Enigma*, Milton Keynes, Authentic Media.

Wilson, I. (2010) *The Shroud: Fresh Light on the 2000-Year-Old Mystery*, London, Transworld.

Printed in Great Britain
by Amazon